Opening up Genesis

KURT STRASSNER

DayOne

Sound and well-written books like this by our ministry friend (and Creation Museum neighbor) Kurt Strassner are desperately needed today, for the church by and large has compromised on the foundational book of the Bible: Genesis.

In a uniquely practical way, Kurt has unpacked the truths of Genesis, the book of the Bible most under attack of all sixty-six books of Scripture and which is often dismissed by theologians and pastors as allegory or even myth. He shows that Genesis is the foundational book for all Christian doctrine and that it must be defended against compromise, otherwise the Bible's foundations are undermined.

Ken Ham

President of the Creation Museum, Petersburg, Kentucky, USA, and Answers in Genesis

Kurt Strassner is an excellent writer and it shows in this commentary on the foundational book of the Bible. He has an easy-to-read style which is lucid, thought-provoking, and contains much practical application. His grasp of God's omnipotent creation is most refreshing. The illustrations he uses for the Flood and for the fire that came on Sodom and Gomorrah are powerful. Later on in Genesis, he searches the mind of Joseph. Just what motivated Joseph as he gave his erring brothers a hard time? Kurt's ability to keep to the text, to avoid the obvious and make us think is just what we need.

Erroll Hulse
Associate Pastor, Leeds Reformed Baptist Church, UK, and Editor, *Reformation Today*

This study guide to Genesis has three primary strengths. First and foremost, it shows accurately what Genesis is all about, not simply in summary but in careful detail. This is what thousands of Christians want and sometimes find hard to locate. Second, and almost as important, it is written simply. No one needs to struggle with strange vocabulary and huge sentences in reading this book. This is immensely important in going on with your study. Third, it applies the text to the needs of the reader. Grasping the message of the Bible is not primarily an academic exercise. Pastors and students sometimes forget this. Kurt Strassner has not done so! All in all, you cannot possibly fail to profit from using this fine tool.

Tom Wells

Retired Pastor of The King's Chapel, West Chester, Ohio, USA, and author

Some surprising but true-to-Scripture exegesis and helpful notes give this commentary the edge over other commentaries of its size. Pastor Kurt Strassner is true to the text in Genesis 1–11, emphasizing six-day creation and endorsing God's sovereign work in contrast to naturalistic atheism. He is also devotional in tone, making application to the saved and unsaved alike, as he does not flinch from bringing out the inconsistencies in the lives of some of the greatest people in the Bible. Throughout the book, God's amazing grace, love, and providence are clearly dealt with. Use this commentary for small-group Bible study, quiet-time reflection and sermon preparation.

Revd Ian McNaughton
Pastor, West Worthing Evangelical Church, West Sussex, and Chairman of Answers in Genesis (UK/Europe)

For Anthony,
lover of Jesus and missionary to Ethiopia:
"God meant it for good" (Gen. 50:20)

First printed 2009

ISBN 978-1-84625-159-7

British Library Cataloguing in Publication Data available

Published by Day One Publications

Ryelands Road, Leominster, England, HR6 8NZ

Telephone 01568 613 740 FAX 01568 611 473

email—sales@dayone.co.uk

web site—www.dayone.co.uk

North American e-mail—usasales@dayone.co.uk

North American web site—www.dayonebookstore.com

Printed by Gutenberg Press, Malta

Contents

List of Bible abbreviations

THE OLD TESTAMENT

Gen.	Genesis
Exod.	Exodus
Lev.	Leviticus
Num.	Numbers
Deut.	Deuteronomy
Josh.	Joshua
Judg.	Judges
Ruth	Ruth
1 Sam.	1 Samuel
2 Sam.	2 Samuel
1 Kings	1 Kings
2 Kings	2 Kings
1 Chr.	1 Chronicles
2 Chr.	2 Chronicles
Ezra	Ezra
Neh.	Nehemiah
Esth.	Esther
Job	Job
Ps.	Psalms
Prov.	Proverbs
Eccles.	Ecclesiastes
S.of S.	Song of Solomon
Isa.	Isaiah
Jer.	Jeremiah
Lam.	Lamentations
Ezek.	Ezekiel
Dan.	Daniel
Hosea	Hosea
Joel	Joel
Amos	Amos
Obad.	Obadiah
Jonah	Jonah
Micah	Micah
Nahum	Nahum
Hab.	Habakkuk
Zeph.	Zephaniah
Hag.	Haggai
Zech.	Zechariah
Mal.	Malachi

THE NEW TESTAMENT

Matt.	Matthew
Mark	Mark
Luke	Luke
John	John
Acts	Acts
Rom.	Romans
1 Cor.	1 Corinthians
2 Cor.	2 Corinthians
Gal.	Galatians
Eph.	Ephesians
Phil.	Philippians
Col.	Colossians
1 Thes.	1 Thessalonians
2 Thes.	2 Thessalonians
1 Tim.	1 Timothy
2 Tim.	2 Timothy
Titus	Titus
Philem.	Philemon
Heb.	Hebrews
James	James
1 Peter	1 Peter
2 Peter	2 Peter
1 John	1 John
2 John	2 John
3 John	3 John
Jude	Jude
Rev.	Revelation

Overview

The book of Genesis is aptly named. In this book we find the "genesis," the beginning, of everything that is—everything, we should say, except God. In the first eleven chapters of this opening book of the Bible we find the beginning of the heavens and the earth, the beginning of the human race, and, sadly, the beginning of human sin. But as the story goes on, we may also trace the beginnings of God's plan of salvation! Through a tiny little family with a great many skeletons in its closets, God begins his plan to save the planet, to forgive human sins, and to send a Savior. Though the book does not name him, Genesis begs for a Savior; Genesis promises a Savior; and Genesis, if we read it rightly, can lead us to the Savior of the world—Jesus, the Son of God.

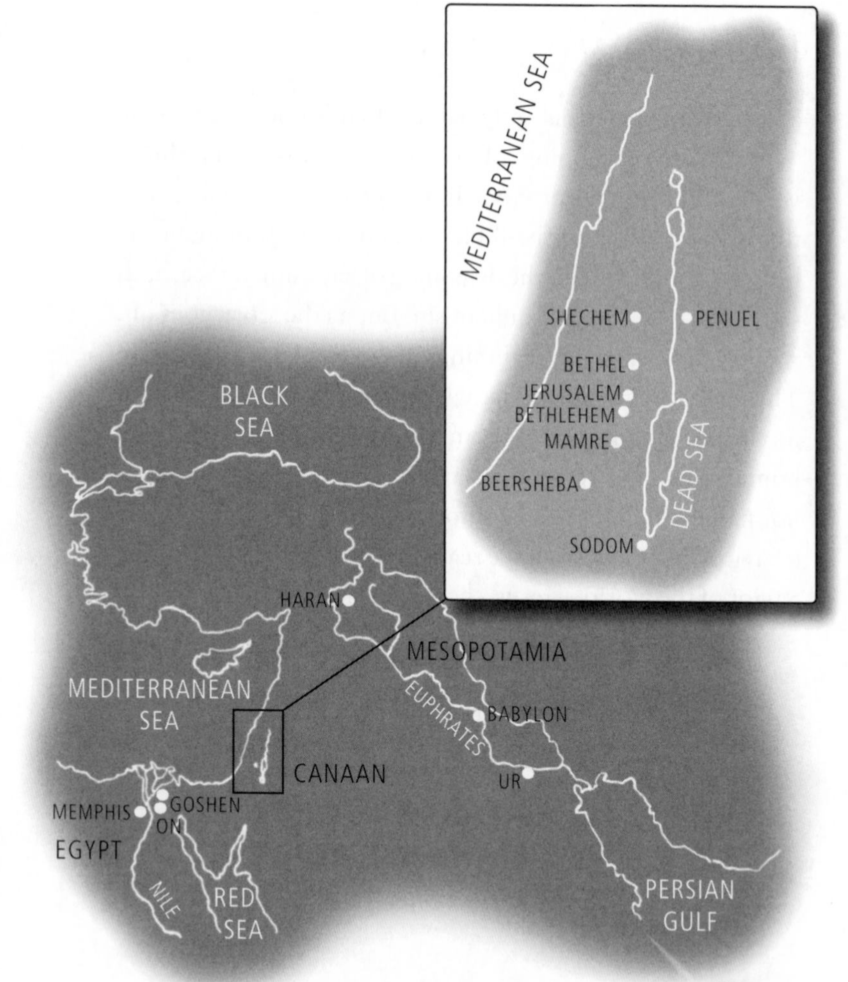

MEDITERRANEAN SEA
SHECHEM
PENUEL
BETHEL
JERUSALEM
BETHLEHEM
MAMRE
DEAD SEA
BEERSHEBA
SODOM

BLACK SEA
HARAN
MESOPOTAMIA
MEDITERRANEAN SEA
EUPHRATES
BABYLON
CANAAN
UR
MEMPHIS
GOSHEN
ON
EGYPT
NILE
RED SEA
PERSIAN GULF

(All dates are approximate.)

6000 BC	2000 BC	1875 BC	1445 BC
CREATION	GOD CALLS ABRAM	ISRAEL RELOCATES TO EGYPT	HEBREW EXODUS FROM EGYPT

Background and summary: The book of beginnings

In the beginning ... God

Genesis is the first book of the Bible, the beginning of everything but God. If we had to give a contemporary English title to this Bible book, we might call it "The book of beginnings," or maybe just "In the beginning." That is what the ancient Hebrews called it: *bereshith*, meaning "In the beginning." The title we use today, "Genesis," comes from the Greek word that means "birth." This book tells the account of how the universe was born.

But there are more beginnings in the book of Genesis. Genesis records the beginning of the *human family*—tracing the family tree all the way back to its roots in Adam and Eve. It depicts the beginning of *sin*, following this polluted river back to its fountainhead in the Garden of Eden. And further, through the family history of Abraham, Isaac, and Jacob—the forefathers of the Messiah, Jesus—Genesis draws up the beginnings, the blueprints, of God's great *plan of salvation* for fallen humanity.

So Genesis teaches us about the beginnings of the world, the human race, the problem of sin, and God's plan of salvation. Each of these themes, which are vitally important in the rest of biblical and human history, finds its origin in this book. That means Genesis is a very significant book, and our study of it will be extremely important for our understanding of our God, of ourselves, of our Bible, and of our world.

Genesis is the book of beginnings. But it is also a book about God. "In the beginning God" is the opening freeze-frame of the Bible. If we try to go back before the world sprang into being, we find God. If we ask where the world came from, Genesis answers: God. If we wonder why the universe continues to operate in an orderly, timely, predictable fashion, the answer in Genesis is God. And as we ponder how all this ancient information has been preserved and passed down to us, the answer again is God, who gave this book to Moses and had him write it down for the ages. So perhaps the best modern title for the book of Genesis would be "In the beginning … God."

How do you see the world?

As I just stated, the book of Genesis will be for us an important component for our understanding of the world in which we live. What you believe (or don't believe) about Genesis is determinative in the development of your worldview. That is because what you do with Genesis largely determines how you answer questions like: Where did the world come from? Where did I come from? What is the purpose for my being on earth? Is there a God? And, if so, what are my responsibilities to him? Why is the world as tangled up as it is? And is there a solution?

How a person answers those questions forms the foundation for the worldview—the basic approach to life—that he or she holds. And if we want to think honestly about which worldview is right, we must take seriously the book of Genesis. Furthermore, if we want to persuade our friends that the biblical, God-centered worldview is the correct worldview, we must understand Genesis and be able to dialogue intelligently with them about it.

If that seems far-fetched, just think through Genesis chapter 1 for a moment. From the very first page of the Bible we may directly address hot-button issues like evolution, the sanctity of human life (i.e. abortion and euthanasia), and the relationship between the sexes. What you believe about Genesis chapter 1 will go a long way in determining how you deal with those issues that are so important in our world at the present moment. The same applies to your understanding of the rest of Genesis. The origin of the world, the question of race, the nature of science—all these questions find wonderful answers in the book of Genesis!

How do you read the Bible?

What you believe about Genesis, and how familiar you are with it, decisively shapes your worldview. And your understanding of Genesis also goes a long way towards determining how well you understand the rest of the Bible. What, really, is sin—and why is it so bad? What does Paul mean when he styles Jesus as the second Adam (Rom. 5)? Was God's sending of his Son merely a reaction to human sin? Or was this the plan all along? Is the idea of a Trinity simply a New Testament realization? Who was this Abraham who is mentioned so often as an example of faith (Rom. 4; Heb. 11; etc.)? And what was Jesus talking about when he urged his

What you believe about Genesis, and how familiar you are with it, decisively shapes your worldview.

disciples to "remember Lot's wife" (Luke 17:32)? All these Bible questions, and more, can only be fully answered by opening up Genesis.

Featuring ...

Genesis is the account of beginnings—one that impacts our entire worldview and our understanding of the Bible as a whole. But who are its main characters?

Well, the list must begin with *God*. After all, he is the one who begins, ends, and carries along this magnificent history. He spoke the universe into being. He declared it all good. He looked on as mankind rebelled. He pronounced both the curse on mankind and the promise to redeem us. He presided over the Flood. He rescued Noah. He called Abraham to be the father of many nations. He led him to the land of Canaan. He kept the chosen family tree alive through the miraculous birth of Isaac. He blessed Jacob and made his family into a great nation. And he did it all for his own glory. So, the primary character in the book of Genesis is none other than God.

The first human character we will encounter is, obviously, *Adam* (chapters 1–3)—the first human being, made from the dust of the ground; placed in authority over God's good earth; given a wife to be his helper; communing unhindered with God; but eventually falling into sin and birthing a race of men and women bent on repeating his folly.

One of the most memorable characters in Genesis is *Noah* (chapters 6–9). A sinner like us, Noah "found favor in the eyes of the LORD" (6:8). When the fallout of Adam's sin had become too great to tolerate, and God was planning a worldwide flood to cleanse the earth, he let Noah in on his plan. He gave him plans for a giant ship. And he kept Noah and his family safe inside that ark while the rest of the world perished. Noah, then, like Adam, became a single seed to which all subsequent human beings can trace their family tree.

God's plan to rescue humankind eventually shifted from Noah to *Abram* (later Abraham; chapters 12–23). God called this Mesopotamian man to become the father of a great nation, sent him on a pilgrimage to that nation's future home, and gave him and his ninety-year-old wife a miracle baby to get the family started. In his trust of God's promise, in his obedience to God's sometimes strange instructions, and in his willingness to go wherever God called him, Abraham became, for every generation since, the supreme example of what it means to have faith in God.

Abraham's son was *Isaac* (chapters 21–27). Also a man of faith, Isaac followed the LORD after his father Abraham, and gave birth to a son who was destined to carry on the lineage of God's chosen nation.

Isaac's son was *Jacob* (chapters 25–36). A one-time rebellious teen who deceived his father, stole from his brother, and dishonored his father-in-law, the younger son of Isaac would eventually meet God face to face and be forever changed. Even his name was changed to "Israel," from which the chosen nation eventually drew its name.

Jacob had twelve sons. Genesis 37–50 focuses our attention on the eleventh of the twelve—*Joseph*. A bit of a problem child like his father, Joseph was taken by God through a serious of difficult providences, each of which serves to teach us how faithful the Lord is to work all things together for the good of his people—both for individuals, like Joseph, and for his people as a whole. Though he couldn't see it, Joseph's individual struggles set the stage for his entire family (the whole, tiny nation of Israel) to be preserved and protected, ultimately preparing the way for the most important human character in the book of Genesis ...

Jesus. Jesus is a character in the book of Genesis? Absolutely! In the days following his resurrection (thousands of years after the events recorded in Genesis), Jesus walked unrecognized along a road with two befuddled Christians. Seeing their distress over the death of their would-be Messiah, Jesus, "beginning with Moses ... explained to them the things concerning Himself in all the Scriptures" (Luke 24:27). As we walk through its pages, we will see how, through the characters and accounts it records, this first book of Moses prophesies of Jesus, typifies Jesus, foreshadows Jesus, prepares the ancestral way for Jesus, and shows us our need of Jesus. My hope, then, is that this book will serve in the spirit of John the Baptist—crying out in the wilderness and shame that we encounter in Genesis, "Prepare the way for Jesus, the Lord!"

May God grant you his blessing as you study his Word and look for his Son!

Part 1
Paradise lost

(1:1–11:32)

1 In the beginning God …

(1:1–2:25)

If Genesis is the book of beginnings, how important is the beginning of that book? Genesis chapters 1 and 2 lay foundations that are vital for understanding all of life. What is God like? Where did we come from? What are we here for? In these first two chapters of the Bible, spanning just seven twenty-four-hour days, we have profound answers to these questions, and more.

Forming and filling

"In the beginning God created the heavens and the earth" (1:1)—light and land, sunshine and sea, forests and fish, and human beings. God made it all in six days. You can remember the order of things by keeping two words in mind: *forming* and *filling*. On days one through three, God *formed* the heavens and the earth. And on days four through six, he *filled* the heavens and the earth with inhabitants. Follow the pattern through:

- On the first day, God created light and separated it from darkness (1:3–5).
- On the second day, he formed the sky—the "expanse," or "firmament" (1:6–8).
- On the third day, he formed the dry land and all its vegetation (1:9–13).
- On the fourth day, God filled the sky with sun, moon, and stars (1:14–19).
- On the fifth day, he filled the waters with fish and sea creatures, and the sky with birds (1:20–23).
- On the sixth day, he filled the land with mammals, reptiles, and, finally, with man (1:24–31).

And "By the seventh day God completed His work which He had done, and He rested on the seventh day from all His work which He had done" (2:2). Observing this pattern, we should find it no surprise that nearly every human civilization from that time until today has ordered its life around a seven-day week—even though most of them have had neither the book of Genesis nor significant contact with one another. This is a testimony, written on the human conscience, of the truthfulness of the biblical creation account.

Evolution and the Bible

Having made mention of the truthfulness of this account, let us say a brief word about evolution. Note that the evolutionary hypothesis is simply that—a *hypothesis*, not scientific fact. Because of the time that has elapsed between the beginning of time and today, no hypothesis of the origins of the world can ever be properly tested, much less proven. So, though many around us are enamored of the evolutionary hypothesis, let us not get carried away by accusations claiming the Bible contradicts proven science. For not only can the evolutionary hypothesis not be scientifically tested or proven, it also cannot, by any reasonable means, be partnered with the biblical creation account. Notice three reasons why:

- First, we are given no reason to believe that the six days of creation were not six literal days. Yes, "with the Lord one day is like a thousand years, and a thousand years like one day" (2 Peter 3:8). But Genesis 1 says again and again that on each day "there was evening and there was morning." That doesn't describe a millennium, but the normal sequence of one twenty-four-hour day!
- Second, notice that the Bible makes it clear that the plants (1:11–12), the sea creatures (1:21), the birds (1:21), the mammals (1:24), and the reptiles (1:24) were all created "after their kind." So what we are being told is this: God did not create an amoeba that turned into a fish. Nor did he create a monkey that evolved into a modern man. Each creature was created as a distinct "kind"!
- Third, notice that man was created in the image of God. Anyone, then, who says that we came from the apes must also be prepared to say that God, in whose image we are made, must be like an ape—or, at least, that God must have been ape-like when he created Adam (maybe he's evolving too?)! Do you see? Evolution

is, at best, silliness; and, at worst, blasphemy! From the very beginning we see the first man, Adam, with God-like characteristics such as speech, reason, creativity, and moral consciousness. Man was made, from the beginning, in the image of God![1]

Up close and personal

Having created Adam in his own image, "the LORD God planted a garden toward the east, in Eden; and there He placed the man whom He had formed" (2:8). The Garden of Eden was specially designed with Adam in mind. It was a home perfectly suited to Adam's needs and capabilities—a reminder that it is a kind and loving God with whom we have to do.

Think about the goodness of the home God provided for Adam. Eden was a bountiful land situated on a river delta (2:10), where the soil would have been rich and black like that in the cotton fields of northwest Mississippi. It was covered with the most beautiful orchards and the most sumptuous fruits (2:9)—apples, oranges, kiwis, plums, and peaches, all growing in Adam's backyard. And the surrounding territory was rich in natural resources (2:12)—gold and onyx for beauty, aromatic gum ("bdellium") for creativity and industry.

Imagine a landscape unspoiled by human "progress," unlimited by climatic conditions, and untainted by sin's curse. That was Adam's home—a home of which we can only dream in the present age but await eagerly in the age to come—a paradise! In this paradise, Adam had free reign. He could live anywhere he wanted; use anything he wanted; and eat anything he wanted, with only one restriction: "from the tree of the knowledge of good and evil you shall not eat, for in the day that you eat from it you will surely die" (2:17).

"Then the LORD God said, 'It is not good for the man to be alone; I will make him a helper suitable for him'" (2:18). Adam and Eve were different, but with a glorious purpose—that the two might fit together like hook and eye. Eve was a "suitable" companion. Perhaps Matthew Henry, the Puritan Bible commentator, said it best: "The woman was made of a rib out of the side of Adam; not made out of his head to rule over him, nor out of his feet to be trampled upon by him, but out of his side to be equal with him, under his arm to be protected by him, and near his heart to be beloved."[2]

This is why it is important (and good!) for a man to "leave his father and his mother, and be joined to his wife" (2:24). Marriage, and healthy marriage in particular, is vitally important as a sign of obedience to God, as a building block for culture, and (most of all) as a beautiful and accurate portrait of the relationship between Christ and his church (Eph. 5:22–33).

In the image of God he created them

Both Adam and Eve were created in the image of God (1:27) and, as our first parents, have a great deal to teach us about what it means to be human. Observe the distinct traits of humanity that Genesis 1 and 2 set forth.

Dignity

If man is created "in the image of God," no one has the right to degrade or destroy human life—neither one's own life, nor that of another. This principle must be applied in the areas of social justice, race relations, sexual ethics, abortion, euthanasia, and a whole host of other topics.

If man is created "in the image of God," no one has the right to degrade or destroy human life—neither one's own life, nor that of another.

Dominion

We are to "rule over" the other created beings (1:26) and "subdue" the earth (1:28). Man has been given dominion over both herbage (2:15) and animals (2:20). Human beings have the God-given authority to chop down trees, build buildings, domesticate animals, and eat meat. Human beings also have the responsibility to do those things responsibly.

Distinction

"Male and female He created them" (1:27). Genesis 2 highlights this difference by giving the genders separate names (2:23), showing how they were created separately (2:7, 22), and calling one a "helper" for the other (2:18). Man and woman were created equal "in the image of God," but their roles are clearly distinct.

Duty

Notice that the first thing God did after creating Adam and Eve was to bless them and give them a command: "Be fruitful and multiply, and fill the earth, and subdue it" (1:28). The relationship between God and man was not one between equals. Nor was it one of autonomy. Man is dependent upon God for the blessings of life and sustenance; and man is accountable to God in the areas of service and obedience! Further, God's command concerning the tree (2:16–17) makes it clear that man was and is capable of receiving and understanding moral instruction—and is responsible for his obedience. If we disobey God, we "will surely die" (2:17).

God created the heavens and the earth

Having fixed our eyes on the origin of man, let us not pass over what is most important—that the origin of man (indeed, the origin of all things) is none other than God! And, as we noted earlier in the Background and Summary chapter, Genesis is preeminently a book about God! So what do Genesis 1 and 2 teach us about the most important subject of all? We see that God is …

Pre-existent

"In the beginning God …" Before the world was, there was God. One of the most basic truths about God is that, without beginning or end, God simply *is*. Nearly every child eventually asks, "Where did God come from?" And Genesis 1:1 gives the answer. God came from nowhere. God simply *is*!

Powerful

As you read chapter 1 you will notice that verses 3, 6, 9, 11, 14, 20, and 24 all begin with the same three English words: "Then God said …" And every time God said something, things happened! "God said, 'Let there be light'; and there was light." "God said, '… let the dry land appear'; and it was so." It feels powerful to say "post office" and have the GPS system in the car listen and act accordingly. But God sits in the driver's seat of a voice-activated *universe*! God is powerful!

Perfect

Everything God does is good. That's what 1:4, 10, 12, 18, 21, 25, and 31 say! Everything God made was "good." The light was good (v. 4). The seas were good (v. 10). The plants were good (v. 12), and so on. God never makes mistakes—even when he allows calamities to strike cities and heartaches to strike individuals. "And we know that God causes all things to work together for good to those who love God, to those who are called according to His purpose" (Rom. 8:28).

Profound

God is glorious! Every good thing God created came from the overflow of his own beauty. Imagine the first six days on planet Earth! Oak trees, tulips, cows, dolphins, giraffes, snapdragons, ponds, mountains, and rivers were springing to life out of nowhere. And even now, God still splashes flowers on the mountainsides; he paints the sky blue, then red, then purple; he makes the waters teem with aquatic life; he fashions perfectly-formed little babies in the womb—all as an outward demonstration of his own creativity and beauty. When we look at the beautiful things God has made, we are to think to ourselves, "If the creation is that glorious, how beautiful must the Creator be!"

Plural

Everywhere we turn in the Bible, it teaches us that there is only one true God (Deut. 6:4, for instance). We must affirm and uphold this truth along with all true Christians. But the Bible also teaches that the one true God is a plural God—and not just in the New Testament, but in the Old as well: "Then God said, 'Let *Us* make man in *Our* image, according to *Our* likeness'" (1:26).[3] God, from the very opening page of the Bible, has revealed himself as both one and more than one. How can that be? The mystery is great, but this is what the Bible teaches.

All things have been created through him and for him

When we turn to the New Testament, we get an even better idea of what God's plurality looks like. The New Testament makes it plain that the one true God exists in three distinct persons—the Father, the Son, and the Holy Spirit. Specifically, it says of Jesus, the Son, "in Him all the fullness of Deity dwells in bodily form" (Col. 2:9); and that "all things have been created through Him and for Him" (Col. 1:16). What a profound truth to read back into Genesis 1:1!

All the "things" of Genesis 1–2 were created by God the Son and for God the Son! That includes each one of us. We owe Jesus our very lives! And this amazing account of creation ought, even more, to motivate us to love him with all our hearts and obey him with all our might. But when we are honest with ourselves, we will admit that none of us does so. Not one of us honors our Creator as we ought (Rom. 1:21). And thus we all stand as guilty sinners before a perfect God and, apart from divine intervention, we "will surely die."

But thank God that the Christ of creation is also the Christ of the cross! Thank God that the Sovereign to whom we are accountable is also the Savior who paid the penalty for our sins! Let us be sure, as we contemplate the Christ of creation, that we also place our trust in him as the Christ of the cross!

For further study ▶

FOR FURTHER STUDY

1. Do some research on the scientific "problems" created by Genesis 1. Are there logical solutions? Can we use scientific defenses of Genesis 1–11 in our witness for Christ? Visit answersingenesis.org.
2. God is one, yet three. How would you explain and defend this biblically for a friend? What Scripture passages would you use?
3. Do a study of marriage in the Bible. What are some of the reasons given for God's creation of it? Which do you think is most important?

TO THINK ABOUT AND DISCUSS

1. Everyone has a worldview (a mental framework that answers questions such as: Where did I come from? What am I doing here? Is there a God? What are my responsibilities to him? How should mankind live?). What are some of the significant ways in which Genesis 1–2 shapes a Christian worldview?
2. What effect will the denial of the historicity of Genesis 1–11 have on: Christian morality? Christian worship? evangelism?
3. Compare Genesis 2:18 with 1 Corinthians 7:25–35. How should a person determine whether to remain single or get married? What are some of the reasons why God said "It is not good for … man to be alone"? In what cases would it be good to be alone?
4. Read John 1:1–18. How does Genesis 1–2 help us appreciate and love Jesus?

2 Paradise lost

(3:1–5:32)

The closing thought of Genesis 2 was: "the man and his wife were both naked and were not ashamed." These words remind us that the Garden of Eden was a place of beauty; a place of bounty; and a place completely unmarred by sin and its crippling, polluting, heartbreaking effects. It was the birthplace of marital intimacy and of intimacy with almighty God. Everything, says God, was "good." Adam and Eve's world was a paradise.

But if Genesis 1–2 was paradise, then, sadly, Genesis 3 and what follows is a description of paradise lost. Through one foolish and rebellious act—eating the fruit God had forbidden—Adam and Eve lost their innocence, their dignity, their home, and their perfect relationship with God. And so, says Romans 5:12, did you and I: "through one man sin entered into the world, and death through sin, and so death spread to all men, because all sinned." The reason we are the way we are—diseased, discontent, disobedient, disappointed, and disenfranchised from God—is because each one of us has inherited a sin sickness and a death sentence from Adam, our first father. How did it happen?

The father of lies

Paradise lost began with the lies of "the serpent"—"the serpent of old who is called the devil and Satan, who deceives the whole world" (Rev. 12:9). Jesus called him "the father of lies" and said that lying is his native language (John 8:44)! So it is no surprise that, in his very first speaking part, we find the devil uttering deceit. And, since he is "crafty" (3:1)—since his expertise is crafting lies that sound almost true—we find Eve falling for his schemes. God had said, quite plainly, not to eat of the one tree in the middle of the garden (3:3). But the devil was able, with clever lies, to convince her that she should indeed eat.

Satan is no less cunning today. Therefore, it may be helpful for us to observe his strategies and guard ourselves accordingly. How does Satan craft his lies? Notice how he destroyed Eve. Satan wants to …

Confuse us

"Indeed, has God said …?" was his introductory question for Eve (3:1). Modern paraphrase: "Are you sure that's what God said? Are you certain that is what he meant?" Eve had a perfectly clear commandment from God. But the serpent planted seeds of doubt in her mind. He does the same in our minds: "Maybe that verse doesn't really mean what it looks as if it means. Maybe God doesn't mean for us to take that literally. Maybe ... Maybe ... Maybe ..." Satan's strategy is to make us doubt the reliability and applicability of the clear teachings of Scripture. We must not believe him!

Caricature God

Notice 3:1 again: "has God said, 'You shall not eat from any tree of the garden'?" Of course God hadn't said that! In fact, he said that Adam and Eve *could* eat from any tree of the garden—except the one (2:16–17)! But you see how Satan operates. He twists what God has said. And he takes one small restriction, placed upon us for our good, and makes God out to be a spoilsport. He says things like: "God is always trying to spoil your fun. What's the matter with looking at a little soft porn? After all, you're not hurting anyone." Or, "Why does God care what you do with your money? Doesn't he want you to enjoy life?" In the face of such lies, we must remember that our God is good, no matter how the devil paints him!

Satan takes one small restriction, placed upon us for our good, and makes God out to be a spoilsport.

Salve our consciences

"You surely will not die!" the devil said to Eve in 3:4. Sin isn't that big a deal, the devil tells us. "OK, God said don't eat from the tree. But come now, do you really think he's going to kill you over this? Go ahead. You know he will forgive you." Have you ever heard him talk like that? Don't believe it. The devil is a liar; God hates sin, and "the wages of sin is death" (Rom. 6:23).

Beautify sin

"God knows that in the day you eat from it your eyes will be opened, and you will be like God, knowing good and evil," Satan said of the forbidden fruit (3:5). There was some element of truth to that statement. Adam and Eve, who had never before known evil, would surely know it now! But do you see what Satan was doing? He was convincing Eve that sin would actually enable liberation and self-actualization! And he is still telling the same lies: "Go ahead and separate from your wife. You'll finally be free.' "Go ahead and take out your frustration. You'll feel much better." "Go ahead and vent your anger towards God. It's cathartic." Lies, all lies! Sin will never make you free. Adam and Eve were promised liberation, but instead (3:7) they received shame. They were promised that they would become *like* God, but instead they found themselves (3:8–10) hiding *from* God.

> Adam and Eve were promised that they would become *like* God, but instead they found themselves hiding *from* God.

Sin's seductive promises always turn out to be a mirage! Those relationships we enter against the will of God leave scars that may never fully fade. Those extra trips to the buffet leave us miserable for the rest of the day and place some of us on operating tables. And what about the nicer car, the bigger TV, the latest gadgetry, and the younger wife? All those things grow old and outdated—leaving us just as empty as we were before. Selfishness and sin never keep their promises.

Excuses, excuses

Worse than broken promises and broken dreams, however, is the broken relationship with God with which sin also leaves us. Adam and Eve knew they had rebelled. And they knew there must be consequences. But instead of repentance, observe their response in 3:11–13:

> "Have you eaten from the tree of which I commanded you not to eat?"
>
> The man said, "The woman whom You gave to be with me, she gave me from the tree, and I ate."
>
> Then the LORD God said to the woman, "What is this you have done?"
>
> And the woman said, "The serpent deceived me, and I ate."

Our first parents' response sounds quite contemporary. First, Adam points his finger at God: "The woman *whom you gave me* made me do it." At the same time, he also shifts the blame onto his wife: "*The woman* whom you gave me made me do it." And when God looks to Eve for an explanation, she points to the serpent—"The devil made me do it"!

Blame-shifting is a universal human disease. Ever since Adam and Eve, it has been part of our sinful human nature: "I know I sometimes lose my temper. But that is just the way God made me." "I know I shouldn't talk to my wife that way, but I'm under a lot of stress at work." "I know I shouldn't read these racy romance novels, but my husband isn't exactly a knight in shining armor anymore." But anytime we begin a sentence with "I know I shouldn't … but," we are on dangerous ground. We ought simply to stop with: "I know I shouldn't." God has made himself clearly seen in creation, in the human conscience, and, most of all, in his Word, so that we are "without excuse" (Rom. 1:20) when we sin against him.

The curse

Whether they wanted to admit their sin or not, Adam and Eve's rebellion came with great consequences. They lost their capacity to rightly enjoy God's good gifts. Perfection was replaced with pain (3:16a). A joyful marriage became an unequal partnership (3:16b). Happy cultivation became sweaty toil (3:17). The beautiful garden became a briar patch (3:18). Once-imperishable bodies began slowly to decay and die (3:19). And they were thrust out of their garden home forever (3:22–24). Everything that was once so good was turned on its head. As we read on in the book of Genesis we find that murder, rape, disease, drunkenness, and death were further results of the sin of Adam and Eve. And the world in which we live today is mixed-up and messy because of their original sin.

The curse on Adam and Eve affected everything about them—including their natures. All that God made—including Adam and Eve—was good. But now these two humans became enslaved to sinful cravings. And, like the other effects of the curse, this sinful nature has been inherited by us all: "through the one man's disobedience the many were made sinners" (Rom. 5:19).

Adam's sinful legacy becomes quite obvious when we turn the page to Genesis 4. Adam and Eve had two sons, Cain and Abel (4:1–2). Had their parents obeyed the LORD, all would have been well with these two boys. But things turned out quite differently. One day, both sons brought offerings to the LORD. Abel's offering was pleasing to God, and Cain's was not (4:4–5). Before Adam's first sin, it would have been inconceivable for Cain to have been rejected by God. But now he was. And this rejection led to further behavior that would have seemed impossible just a few years before: murder. So jealous was Cain of his brother that he eventually murdered him (4:8); "through one man [Adam] sin entered into the world" (Rom. 5:12).

Cain became a carbon copy of his sinful father. And Cain is a picture of us all. Why do we find ourselves alienated from God? Why are we weighed down with selfishness, bitterness, envy, and the like? Because we have inherited Adam's sin nature; "through the one man's disobedience the many were made sinners." And, in inheriting Adam's sin nature, we have inherited the death that comes with it. Genesis 5 bears this fact out. "And he died" is the recurring refrain of the chapter and becomes the theme of the human race, from Adam to Seth to Enosh to us. Because Adam sinned, we became sinners. And, because of Adam's sin and our own sin, we have God's sentence of death hanging over our heads—"through one transgression [that of Adam] there resulted condemnation to all men" (Rom. 5:18).

A covering for sin

Now, Genesis 5 isn't all gloomy, is it? Amid the monotony of "So all the days of ____ were ____ years, and he died" comes this twist: "So all the days of Enoch were three hundred and sixty-five years. Enoch walked with God; and he was not, for

God took him" (5:23–24). What a word of hope! Yes, God was true to his word (2:17)—Adam's sin resulted in death for Adam, and in "condemnation to all men" (Rom. 5:19). But Enoch's account reminds us that death is not the final word. There *is* the possibility of redemption in this fallen world!

We get a hint of God's plan of redemption in chapter 3. First, God said that a descendant of this very woman, Eve, would someday be born to crush the serpent's head (3:15). Then, in verse 21, we find that, after all Adam and Eve had done, God was merciful and covered their sins. "The LORD God made garments of skin for Adam and his wife, and clothed them." Isn't that amazing? They deserved to die, yet God forgave their sin and covered their shame!

This covering for sin was sheer grace—a totally free and undeserved gift. But an animal had to die in order for Adam and Eve's sins to be covered. And so it is with us. God offers you and me the same free gift. Yes, the effects of the curse still linger in the air of this life. But God offers us an eternal covering of forgiveness for our sins and our shame. The covering is a gift, free to us, but costing someone his life—namely Jesus, "the Lamb of God who takes away the sin of the world" (John 1:29). He is the covering for our guilt and shame. He is the sacrifice for our sin! "For if by the transgression of the one [Adam], death reigned through the one, much more those who receive the abundance of grace and of the gift of righteousness will reign in life through the One, Jesus Christ" (Rom. 5:17).

Have you come to terms with these facts? Have you come to admit how bad your sin really is? And how badly you need the covering of Jesus? Or are you still, like Adam and Eve, hiding yourself from God? Shifting the blame onto others? Trying to cover your shame with a handful of fig leaves (see 3:7) you've picked up along the way—penance, baptism, church attendance, and so on? It will never work! God knows where to find you when you are hiding. God sees right through the excuses. And God is not impressed with our religious fig leaves.[1] In fact, these attempts to rescue ourselves are not even necessary. God has given us his Son for a covering! When we trust in him, we need no longer hide. When we trust in him, excuses are no longer necessary. When we trust in him, we are clothed in his righteousness. So look to the seed of the woman who has crushed the serpent's head; and behold "the Lamb of God who takes away the sin of the world."

For further study ▶

FOR FURTHER STUDY

1. Why do you think God rejected Cain's offering and accepted Abel's? What was the difference between "an offering … of the fruit of the ground" (4:3) and the "firstlings of [the] flock" (4:4)? What do Cain and Abel teach us about our own service to God? How does Abel's offering foreshadow Jesus?
2. Sin's "desire is for you, but you must master it" (4:7). What does the Bible teach about mastering sin? See Romans 6:1–14.
3. Where else does the Bible speak of Enoch? What do these passages teach us about what it means to walk with God?

TO THINK ABOUT AND DISCUSS

1. Can you think of examples, from your own life, of times when Satan has tried to confuse you, caricature God, or beautify sin? How did you overcome the temptation? How did Jesus overcome such temptations? See Matthew 4.
2. What are some common locations onto which we Westerners tend to shift our blame? Are you tempted to blame any of these people, events, or phenomena when you sin? What is the biblical perspective on these things?
3. Does it seem "fair" that Adam's sin results in condemnation to us all? If we choose to reject the idea that we are born condemned because of Adam, what bearing does that have on our understanding of the gospel? See Romans 5:12–21.

3 If it keeps on raining …

(6:1–9:29)

In my city, Cincinnati, we speak about the great flood of 1997, and the even greater flood of 1937, when the waters of the Ohio River made the streets of downtown Cincinnati look like the canals of Venice. Every few years, we have a significant flood. So we name them—"the flood of '37," "the flood of '97"—to distinguish one from another. But the flood spoken of in Genesis 6–9 needs no such signature. So wide was it spread, so colossal was the destruction, so well is it known that we simply call it "the Flood."

The account of Noah and the Flood covers four chapters in Genesis. But the basic details are sketched for us in Genesis 6:1–8, upon which we will focus the attention of this chapter.

Only evil continually

Genesis 6 begins with a big problem—the intermarriage

of families of God-fearing people ("the sons of God")[1] with families of unbelievers ("the daughters of men," v. 2). Young men who were believers in the LORD began to marry "whomever they chose." The result was moral chaos. By the time we reach verse 5, we find there was no longer any distinction between the religious and the irreligious: "the LORD saw that the wickedness of man was great on the earth, and that every intent of the thoughts of his heart was only evil continually."

For all the good that homeless shelters, cancer research, or AIDS orphanages will do on this earth, those efforts will not carry over to eternity unless they are done in the name of the God and Father of our Lord Jesus Christ.

"Only evil continually." Now that is a perfect description of unredeemed men and women of any era—including our own. Human beings are not basically good. Because of the curse brought about by Adam's sin (see Gen. 3 and Rom. 5), human beings are basically bad—completely sinful. How can I say such a thing? We can look around the world and see good things being attempted and noble tasks being achieved. But the problem is not simply with our attempts and our achievements. The problem is with our hearts. Until we come to bow the knee to Jesus Christ as King of the universe, our own agendas remain on the thrones of our hearts—we are without God in the world. And that means that even our best acts are godless acts. And for all the good that homeless shelters, cancer research, or AIDS orphanages will do on this earth, those efforts will not carry over to eternity unless they are done in the name of the God and Father of our Lord Jesus Christ.

To put it another way: if our hearts are godless, then even our most altruistic deeds are filthy rags because they are done by our own self-effort and not through the strength that God supplies. And that, even in the most loving and giving among us, leads to secret pride: "Look at what *I* achieved"; "Look at who *we* helped"; "Look at what *mankind* has accomplished." And in that kind of thinking, subtle or unspoken as it may be, there is a robbery of the glory of God who made us and who alone gives us the ability to accomplish what is meaningful.

Some of us do "only evil continually" by blatantly rebelling against God. Others of us do "only evil continually" by failing to acknowledge God as the giver of every good and perfect gift—including the gifts we ourselves give to others. But both lifestyles are equally godless and, as we shall see, worthy of judgment.

The LORD was sorry he had made man

The continual sin of mankind in Genesis 6:5 leads to one of the most startling sentences in the Bible in Genesis 6:6: "The LORD was sorry that He had made man on the earth, and He was grieved in His heart." If this were not recorded for us in Holy Scripture, it would almost sound unbelievable! Just a few chapters ago, God was creating man in his own image and calling him "good." And now we read that he was "sorry that He had made" him! Think of that the next time you are tempted to brush God aside through sin.

"The LORD was sorry that He had made man." This is not the regret you feel when you realize you have made a mistake. God never makes mistakes. So verse 6 is not a picture of God wringing his hands over a bad decision. But it *is* a picture of a God who is genuinely sorry.

How can a God who never makes mistakes be sorry over something he did? When *we* say that we are sorry about something, what we usually mean is: "I wish it never happened." But there are times when we may do what is best and yet be sorrowful about doing it—such as when we discipline our children or confront a brother or sister in sin. Most of us are sorry that we sometimes have to do these things. But, at the same time, we know that they are the right things to do. My emotions may be sorry for having to discipline my children. But my mind and will know it is the right thing to do. So I do it sorrowfully, but with no regrets.

This is how we explain Genesis 6:6. On the level of his divine will, God knew that creation was no mistake. But on the level of his emotions, the way man turned out brought great sorrow. So God could say, with all honesty, that he was "sorry that He had made man," and yet still be the God who never makes a mistake.

Now, the fact that we have to take several paragraphs to untangle verse 6 is significant. We have rightly taken time to understand it because it is such a weighty verse. God was truly sorry that he had made man. His heart is broken over men and women who choose to live without him, rebelling against his laws and ignoring his kindness.

I will blot man from the face of the land

Now, not only was God grieved over sin—he was also angry. And that anger was so just and so deep that "The LORD said, 'I will blot out man whom I have created from the face of the land'" (6:7). God was going to wipe mankind completely off the face of the earth, as a housewife scrapes the filthy black crud from the inside of her oven. The whole earth had become, and continues to be, "corrupt in the sight of God" (6:11).

"I will blot out man ... from the face of the land." The fulfillment of this promise is described in chapter 7. God caused waters to burst forth, not only from the clouds, but also from the belly of the earth (7:11). The earth was inundated with water for forty days and nights (7:12). So much water was there that the highest mountains were covered (7:19). And "all in whose nostrils was the breath of life, died" (7:22)—including nearly the entire human race. God had done what he said he would do—"blot out man ... from the face of the land."

Noah found favor with God

The ancient world, like our own, deserved the judgment of God. But amid the ugliness of sin, and the promise of judgment, we read these wonderful sentences (6:8–9): "But Noah found favor in the eyes of the LORD ... Noah was a righteous man, blameless in his time; Noah walked with God."

Reading those verses, we could now launch into a nice "be like Noah" sermon—like those that many of us heard as children. But that is not the point of the passage. The thrust of this chapter is not that Noah was good, but that God is gracious. Look closely at verse 8: "Noah found *favor* in the eyes of the LORD." The word translated "favor" here is the Hebrew word that means "grace." Noah found grace—free, unmerited kindness—in the eyes of the LORD. Noah was righteous and blameless, yes. But he wasn't naturally so. By nature, Noah was a born sinner—just look at him sprawled out drunk and naked on his living room floor at the end of chapter 9! The curse of Adam had fallen as heavily on Noah as it had on anyone else. So the only reason Noah was "blameless in his time" was because God had shown him "favor"!

The curse of Adam had fallen as heavily on Noah as it had on anyone else. So the only reason Noah was "blameless in his time" was because God had shown him "favor"!

The remarkable thing about verses 8–9 is not Noah's goodness, but God's "favor"—God's grace! The effect of verse 8, then, is to say: The whole earth was wicked but, of his own free will, God decided to show undeserved kindness to Noah! Now, how did he do it?

Well, in Genesis 6:13–22, God gave Noah specific instructions for the construction of an ark—a mighty ship that would provide safe haven for Noah, for his family, for all the various kinds of animals, and for anyone else who was willing to join them on board. So Noah built the ark as he had been told (6:22) and readied himself and his family to enter the ark. And, when the rains came and the world perished, Noah, sinner though he was, was saved. "Noah found favor"—undeserved grace—"in the eyes of the LORD."

Jesus, our ark

The account of Noah's finding favor with God is a beautiful foreshadowing of the gospel of Jesus Christ. The gospel says that man is still as sinful as he ever was—"there is none righteous, not even one" (Rom. 3:10). The gospel says that, one day, God is going to destroy all flesh again—this time by fire (2 Peter 3:10). But the gospel also says that, just as he did in the days of Noah, God has provided us with a way of escape—an ark—in the person of Jesus Christ. In Jesus—who lived a sinless life, died in our place, and rose on the third day—we, like Noah, may find "favor in the eyes of the LORD."

Yes, as detailed as was God's plan for Noah's ark—the wood, the pitch, the dimensions, the windows and doors (6:14–21)—he laid down the plans for the thirty-three-year life of his Son with much more care! In his premeditated mercy, God planned out every detail of the life of Jesus so as to provide us with a perfect Savior, with an ark that will not sink! And "whoever believes in Him will not be disappointed" (Rom. 10:11)!

So we close this chapter with another reminder to climb on board the ark. God has fixed his day of judgment. The sands of time are sinking. The day of judgment draws ever closer. And in that day, God will not relent of his fury. But while he tarries, we live, like Noah, in an age of "favor." We live under the offer of complete rescue from the wrath to come. So let us heed

God's warning before the rains come. While Noah preached to his contemporaries (2 Peter 2:5), they had opportunity to climb aboard the ark and be saved. But they missed the opportunity of grace. Let us be sure not to imitate them. Let us rather imitate Noah in trusting God and doing "according to all that God had commanded him" (6:22). Let us climb aboard the security and safety of Jesus Christ, our ark!

FOR FURTHER STUDY

1. Many modern critics question the factual reality of the biblical Flood account. Do some research (biblical, historical, and scientific) that will equip you to defend the veracity of the biblical Flood account. You might begin with answersingenesis.org, and consult some more lengthy commentaries on the book of Genesis.
2. In describing God's rescue of Noah and his family, Genesis 8 begins with the phrase "But God." Do a word search on this phrase. How often is it found in the Bible? In what circumstances? What does it often teach us about God?
3. In 8:21–22, God made a covenant with Noah never again to destroy the earth with water. Research the other covenants God made in the Old Testament—with Abraham, Moses, and David. How are they similar to, and how do they differ from, the covenant God has made with us in Christ?

TO THINK ABOUT AND DISCUSS

1. Why do you suppose that many folk consider the Flood account to be a mere fable? Why would secular people view it this way? Why do you think that some within church circles do the same?
2. In 2 Peter 2:5, Peter calls Noah a "preacher of righteousness." What do you think Noah was preaching about? What implications does 2 Peter 2:5 have on how we who have climbed aboard Jesus, our ark, should behave towards those still "on land"?

4 Stairway to heaven

(10:1–11:32)

I have a keen interest in geography and maps. At my bedside are usually four books: my Bible, a copy of whichever Christian book I am reading, the *National Geographic Atlas of the World*, and a *Rand McNally Road Atlas*. Guests in our home often find me sliding back to the bedroom to "bring out the maps" and look up some particular place that may have come up in conversation. So many different people in so many different places ... and they all date back to Genesis 10–11!

The table of nations

At first glance, Genesis 10 appears simply to be a bland genealogical record of Noah's family. But these thirty-two verses of genealogy are, in fact, a table of the many nations and people groups founded by the family of Noah after the Flood. Without being overly tedious, let us notice just a few of the geographical implications of this chapter:[1]

- Japheth, Noah's youngest son, and his descendants (10:2–5) were largely responsible for the founding of much of what is now Eastern Europe. Some of the settlements included Ukraine (Gomer), Turkey (Magog, Tubal, Meshech), Greece (Javan), southern Russia (Ashkenaz), Cyprus (Elishah), and the Greek Isles (Kittim).
- Ham, Noah's middle child, and his descendants (10:6–19) are the ancestors of many of the peoples of North Africa and the Middle East—all along the southern and eastern coasts of the Mediterranean Sea. The nations settled by Ham include Sudan (Cush), Egypt (Mizraim), Libya (Put), Yemen (Sheba), Lebanon (Sidon), and Palestine (Canaan).
- Finally, Shem, Noah's firstborn, and his descendants (10:21–31) grew into the dominant nations of the Middle East. They settled in regions like modern Iran (Elam), Iraq (Asshur), Assyria (Aram), and Saudi Arabia (Joktan). Most significantly, Eber settled in Ancient Mesopotamia and, through his descendants Abraham, Isaac, and Jacob, fathered the nation of Israel. In fact, the designation "Hebrew" is probably a derivative of the name Eber.

So, as you can see, with a little research, Genesis chapter 10 could be a map-lover's dream. But this is more than just interesting geographical history. It is also a very sensible explanation of how the world began to go from a post-Flood frontier inhabited by only eight people to the diversely populated planet that it is today. Here also is a reminder that God knows and cares for the nations and peoples of this earth by name; a foreshadowing of God's promise to one day gather people from every tongue, tribe, people, and nation into his kingdom through Jesus. He spread them out so that he might bring them back in! That is what Acts 17:26–27 says: "He made from one man every nation of mankind to live on all the face of the earth, having determined their appointed times and the boundaries of their habitation, *that they would seek God*."

God created and loves the diversity of the nations. He desires that heaven be a beautiful mosaic of human culture and language praising his Son. In fact, this global diversification plan, which we see coming to fruition in Genesis 10, was God's plan from the beginning (see Gen. 1:28). But, in chapter 11, we discover there was also a more immediate, and less encouraging, reason for the dispersal of Noah's descendants.

The tower of Babel

The account of the tower of Babel (11:1–9) is one of the saddest and most momentous stories in the Bible—sad because of the rebellion it depicts; momentous because of the world cultures that it spawned. Let's think through the account in four parts:

Rebellion

There is nothing inherently wrong with building a tower. In fact, it must have seemed like a great idea. After all, Babel was surely a feat of architectural beauty. And it was bringing people together in a common cause. So what could have been so wrong?

Well, we must remember Genesis 9:1, when God instructed mankind, through Noah, to “Be fruitful and multiply, and fill the earth.” And again in 9:7 he told them to “Populate the earth abundantly and multiply in it.” God’s instructions were clear. The people were not to hunker down in one spot. They were to spread out over the whole earth! But listen to 11:1–2: “Now the whole earth used the same language and the same words. It came about as they journeyed east, that they found a plain in the land of Shinar and settled there.”

What was so wrong with the tower of Babel? First, that there never should have been a Babel! There never should have been this gathering together of the earth’s population in the first place. The people had done what seemed convenient instead of what was commanded! It seemed much wiser to congregate together in one large metropolis than to be “scattered abroad over the face of the whole earth” (v. 4). So they ignored God’s clear instructions in favor of their own wisdom.

Let us admit that modern men and women are not above the ancient sin of Babel—thinking ourselves wiser than God. “Surely God isn’t saying what it looks as if he’s saying,” we think to ourselves. “Surely God will understand if I fudge on this commandment.” “Surely, given the modern situation, we can’t be expected to take all these commands literally.” This is the sin of Babel, and of many a modern churchgoer, too.

Renown

Now, the main reason why the descendants of Noah thought

themselves wiser than God was because they had already deemed themselves more important than God. Notice verse 4 again: "Come, let us build for ourselves a city, and a tower whose top will reach into heaven, and let us make for ourselves a name." Their chief goal had shifted from glorifying God and enjoying him forever to promoting their own renown.

The tower of Babel would have actually been what is called a ziggurat—a stair-stepped, pyramid-shaped edifice. Literally, it was a stairway to heaven; an attempt to gain, by human effort, what only God can give. They thought that, if they could just provide themselves with enough fame and fortune, there would be heaven on earth.

"Let us make for ourselves a name." Isn't that the mantra of our age? It's why we wear what we wear; why we drive what we drive; why pastors long for the bigger and better church. It is why the Pharisees (like some of us) loved to do their religious deeds—to be noticed by men. Self-promotion is simply the air we breathe in the Western world. So we need constantly to ask ourselves: Am I purchasing this item/seeking this promotion/performing this service so that I might feel better about myself/attract attention to myself/live more comfortably for myself? Or am I doing it for the glory of God?

Restraint

In verse 6 God responded to the people's building project: "Behold, they are one people, and they all have the same language. And this is what they began to do, and now nothing which they purpose to do will be impossible for them."

God's response might sound confusing to us. It almost sounds as if he is saying that, should he leave man to himself, he really would be able to build a tower all the way to heaven! But I don't believe that is what is meant here. The phrase "nothing ... will be impossible for them" likely refers, not to the heights of accomplishment that mankind might achieve, but to the depths of sin to which mankind is capable of falling. In other words, "If I let their sin go unchecked, there is no telling how much worse it will get. No rebellion will be too great for them. Nothing will be sacred in their crooked hearts."

Have you realized that about the world? If God had not fenced us about with civil powers, religious influence, and fear of punishment, we could be in as much darkness as the Auca Indians of Ecuador, or worse! Have you realized that about *yourself*? The reason you and I have not gone off the deep end into sin is not because we are morally superior to the terrorists of the world, but because of God's restraining grace. We ought to remember this the next time we read about prostitution in the newspapers or pass a drunk person on the street. We should remember Babel and remind ourselves, "If God doesn't restrain the natural bent of my heart, nothing will be impossible for me."

The reason you and I have not gone off the deep end into sin is not because we are morally superior to the terrorists of the world, but because of God's restraining grace.

Reversal

How did God restrain the evil of Noah's descendants? He scrambled their language (11:7), foiled their plans, and scattered them over the whole face of the earth to make sure that nothing like Babel was attempted again (11:8).

What an ironic reversal of fortunes! They had wanted to make a name for themselves, and now they couldn't pronounce one another's names! They had wanted to ensure that they wouldn't be scattered over the whole face of the earth, but that is exactly what ended up happening. What a reminder that God is opposed to the proud—and will often make the punishment for our arrogance a direct reversal of our prideful intentions! If we have adopted plans without consulting the Lord and his Word, we should not be surprised if we find our dreams turned on their heads. This is cause for reflection when our plans fail. Why has this business deal flopped? Why did that relationship sour? Why did that purchase end up such a waste? The answer may not always be chastisement for sin, but Babel reminds us that it is a possibility.

God has a way of showing us when we have left him out of the equation, hasn't he? But, if we believe, even this is for our good—because it gives us an opportunity to repent. And it teaches us to "Commit [our] works to the LORD" that our "plans will be established" (Prov. 16:3).

The tale of salvation

Genesis 11 concludes by zeroing in on the genealogy of just one of the sons of Noah—Shem (11:10–32). It was through the line of Shem that Abram, the father of the Jewish race, would be born. So here we have the beginning of God's setting apart of the Hebrews as his chosen people. Here we have a wonderful reminder that, amid all the mess of Babel, God remembered mercy and set aside a people to whom he would grant undeserved salvation.

Ultimately, we too are recipients of the same undeserved mercy through the redemption which is in Christ Jesus. And this genealogy is a reminder of *him*, too. If you look at 11:10–32 closely, comparing these verses with Luke 3, you will find that all of these names are repeated by Luke as being ancestors of the Messiah. Isn't that wonderful to know? All the way back in Genesis 11, on the heels of one of the greatest rebellions in human history, God was planning to send his Son! God truly loves sinners—and longs to save them!

Have you been willing to accept that love—admitting that it is undeserved and can never be earned? Have you laid down your rebellion and the desire to make a name for yourself, and admitted that your sufficiency and salvation are found in Christ alone? Or are you, like the ancient people of Babel, trying to build your own little stairway to heaven?

For further study ▶

FOR FURTHER STUDY

1. Trace the teaching about Babel, or Babylon, through the Bible. How is this ancient city usually portrayed? How is its name used symbolically? How does "Babel" still exist today?
2. The scrambling of human language is an important theme in the Babel account. How and where does the Bible come back to this theme? How is the diversification of language redeemed, in the New Testament, by Jesus?

TO THINK ABOUT AND DISCUSS

1. The inhabitants of Babel lived with peculiar "advantages" that made life easier for them and caused them to forget their need for God (a large city, unified language, growing civilization). What modern "advantages" do you enjoy that tempt you to forget your need for God?
2. There was nothing inherently wrong with building a tower, but the people's motivation was wicked. Are there undertakings in your personal life, family, or church which aren't inherently wrong but are arising from wrong motives?

Part 2
Abraham—man of faith

(12:1–23:20)

5 In *you* all the families of the earth will be blessed?

(12:1–14:24)

We have already noted that Genesis may be rightly called "The book of beginnings." In the opening eleven chapters we witnessed the beginning of God's creation, the beginning of the human race, the beginning of marriage and family, and (sadly) the beginning of human sin. The very air we breathe—both literal and figurative air—has its origins in Genesis 1–11.

Now as we open chapter 12, we find that it, too, signals a new beginning. In this chapter we find the earliest shoots in the Jewish family tree. And since "salvation is from the Jews" (John 4:22), Genesis 12 and following offer us the initial blueprints of God's great plan of salvation. When we read about God's calling of Abram, we are not simply given a lesson in history. We are actually tracing a story line that takes us all the way to the Lord Jesus himself. So the calling of Abram—the beginning of the nation of Israel—is a story of tremendous significance.

God's commandment

It had been more than 300 years since Noah's Flood—the last recorded instance of God speaking to mankind. That is a long time to go without hearing a word from the LORD. Some of God's faithful may have begun to think that God had forgotten them; that God had withdrawn from active participation in the affairs of planet Earth. But in 12:1, "the LORD said to Abram ..."!

Here is a word of hope for us! Sometimes God may seem silent. We wonder if he has forgotten us, or, worse yet, laid us aside altogether. But Genesis 12 is a reminder that God never forgets his people. Even after the aggravation and rebellion of Babel, even after three-and-a-half centuries of seeming silence, God had not forgotten his promise to save the world (Gen. 3:15). And, with that plan in mind, God spoke to a man named Abram:

> Go forth from your country,
> And from your relatives
> And from your father's house,
> To the land which I will show you ...

That is a tall order, isn't it? "Abram, I want you to pack up your things and move. I want you to leave behind your homeland, along with the culture and language you've known all your life. I want you to leave your relatives, too. And make sure you gather together all your possessions because you won't ever be coming back to this house your father worked so hard to build for you. I want you to leave it all, Abram—and come and follow me. And by the way, I'm not going to tell you where we're going until we get there." Isn't that what 12:1 says? The task was difficult indeed.

If Abram was anything like most of us, he could have thought of all sorts of excuses and arguments for why he shouldn't go. "Surely the LORD doesn't want me to do *that*. I must have misheard him. God wouldn't ask me to leave everything I've ever known behind. I can obey and serve him just fine right here in beautiful Ur." But what a lesson there is in his obedience! He went forward, not because it made sense; not because it was easy; not because it seemed the most feasible way to raise a family; but simply because God said so! That is the essence of faith (Heb. 11:8)—obedience to God's commandments even when we don't know what obedience will bring.

God's covenant

Abram was given a difficult task in 12:1. But it is important to note that God didn't stop speaking there. In fact, beginning with verse 2, we find that attached to God's difficult commandment was a wonderful covenant—a wonderful blessing should Abram trust and obey:

> And I will make you a great nation,[1]
> And I will bless you,
> And make your name great;
> And so you shall be a blessing …

Now, many of us, had we been in Abram's sandals, might never have heard God's promises at all. After hearing verse 1, we'd have been so engrossed in drawing up our counter-proposal, so busy formulating our excuses, that we would have totally missed everything else God had to say! But Abram didn't stop listening after verse 1! If he had, he might never have obeyed. Because, you see, obedience *to* God always arises out of trust *in* God. In other words, we obey God because we believe that he knows what is best. That is why Bible commands so often seem connected with Bible promises—to help us see that there is reward in earnestly seeking God; that there are blessings in obedience—so that we might be wooed to obey.

Bible commands so often seem connected with Bible promises to help us see that there is reward in earnestly seeking God, that there are blessings in obedience.

Abram was certainly wooed to obey. What great promises God made to him: a great name, a great nation, and a great blessing. And, with the encouragement of these promises, Abram was able to leave all he had ever known and go to a strange place with no prospect of success—except that God had promised to care for him.

It is true that God doesn't always make such specific promises to us. Sometimes all we have to go on is: "God causes all things to work together for good to those who love God" (Rom. 8:28). But that is enough! God promises that, for those who love him—for those who keep his commandments (John 14:15)—their best interests will always be the final result. Sometimes that doesn't happen right away. Abram's 600-mile trek to Egypt was surely no walk in the park! But the end result for him, and for all who trust and obey, would be a good one.

Moving ahead, we need to notice the most important,

most long-term aspect of God's covenant with Abram. We find it in verse 3:

> And I will bless those who bless you,
> And the one who curses you I will curse
> And in you all the families of the earth will be blessed.

What did God mean when he said, "... in you all the families of the earth will be blessed"? Well, Abram couldn't have understood this fully. But as the rest of the Old Testament unfolds we begin to understand that, through the Jews—Abram's family—God was going to send a Savior, whose atoning blood would "sprinkle many nations" (Isa. 52:15). And when we turn over to the New Testament, we find that it is through *Jesus*—the descendant of Abram—that people from "every nation and all tribes and peoples and tongues" (Rev. 7:9) will be redeemed and made God's very own.

What mercy that, after the muddy waters of human sin that necessitated the Flood, and after the confusion of human pride that characterized the tower of Babel, God still had a plan to bless "all the families of the earth"—through Abram, and, ultimately, through his descendant, Jesus! Here among Sarai's boxes and Abram's moving van is another reminder that all the Law and the prophets point us forward to God's Son (Luke 24:27)!

Abram's commitment

Now, wonderful as the promises were, and gracious as God had been, Abram still had to decide whether or not to obey—and thank God he did! In 12:4 we read this simple and wonderful sentence: "So Abram went forth as the LORD had spoken to him." No questions asked. No altering of the plans.

He just got up from his place, packed his bags, and left "as the Lord had spoken to him." And in this regard, Abram is a quintessential example of what it means to walk with God. Because it was the Lord who spoke, and because he trusted God's promise to do him good, Abram simply obeyed.

So we must all ask ourselves, "What about me? Am I simply obeying the Lord? Or are there clear commandments of God that I have left undone? If the latter is true, what is the source of difficulty? Is it that I have yet to call him 'Lord'—have yet to admit that God has ownership rights over my life? Or am I dragging my feet because I'm not quite sure I trust that God will really work things out for my good?" All disobedience boils down to one of the two. Either we do not care what God says (he is not Lord); or we do not believe what God says (we do not trust him).

Am I dragging my feet because I'm not quite sure I trust that God will really work things out for my good?

For the Christian—the person who has come to know God in Christ—the problem is usually one of faith. We struggle to *obey* because we struggle to *believe* that God's way will really work out for the best. So, like Abram, we need to listen to and trust God's promises! "Abram went forth as the Lord had spoken" because he believed that God would do as he said: that he would bless him; that he would care for him; that he wouldn't leave him wandering in the wilderness, but would truly bring him to "the land which I will show you." Abram was also able to give his nephew Lot first dibs in the new land (ch. 13) because he continued to believe that God would bring him to "the land which I will show you." And he was able to show unbelievable kindness to Lot (ch. 14), even after Lot's selfishness, because he knew that it was the LORD who held his destiny in his hands. Abram's simple faith that God really was on his side allowed him to do what was right again and again!

Learn from Abram. God is not stingy! He will not leave you in the desert when once you have obeyed. No! He brought Abram to the promised land, and he will fulfill all his promises to us if we will but trust and obey!

Abram's compromise

Now, sadly (but helpfully), Genesis 12 reminds us that Abram didn't always trust and obey. Verses 10–20 tell the devastating account of how he put Sarai, his wife, in an extremely compromised position. Afraid that the Egyptians might take a liking to her, Abram asked Sarai to pretend to be his sister, so that, should a strong Egyptian man desire her for himself, Abram would be no perceived obstacle to their nuptials. Look at the man of faith now, asking his wife to do this so that "it may go well with me" (12:13). This is a far cry from God's mandate that a husband love his wife and give himself up for her (Eph. 5:25)! And it is a far cry from the Abram we have been admiring so far! He traded in his wife in exchange for "sheep and oxen and donkeys" (12:16).

What had happened to Abram? He momentarily stopped believing what God said in 12:3: "I will bless those who bless you, and the one who curses you I will curse." Believing that would have taken care of any inappropriate advances made towards Abram's wife. But he forgot what God had said. When he arrived in Egypt, instead of trusting the LORD, Abram devised a plan: “Let’s pretend you’re my sister. That should make everything go much more smoothly.”

Now, here is another lesson for us who wish to obey the Lord. If, as we said earlier, our obedience *to* God arises from our faith *in* God, then we are in big trouble the moment we stop trusting in God and start devising our own plans. This Abram did, to his great shame—and his wife’s great hurt.

Can you imagine what the Egyptians might have thought of Abram after this episode? They’d have scoffed at his claim to be God’s chosen one. “God is going to bless *you*? And in *you* all the families of the earth will be blessed? The man who treated his wife in this way? God is going to restore the world through you? Come on, Abram, get serious!” That seems like a logical conclusion, doesn’t it? The ugliness of 12:10–20 seems as if it will undermine all the promises that have gone before.

“God is going to bless *you*?” That’s a reasonable question, isn’t it? It’s one we all could ponder in light of our own sins. We know where we have been. We know what we have done. And when we allow those memories to flash across the movie screens of our minds, we might ask ourselves the very same question: “Look at my life! Why would God pick *me*? Why would he bless *me*? Why would he care for *me*?” These very questions—not thrown at us by our enemies, but eating at us from within our own guilty consciences—can be quite debilitating.

So we need to remember that Abram knew something the Egyptians did not. Abram remembered something that we sometimes forget—that God is not only the God of promise, but also the God of provision! Read what happened after this episode:

> So Abram went up from Egypt to the Negev, he and his wife and all that belonged to him, and Lot with him. Now Abram was very rich in livestock, in silver and in gold. He went on his journeys from the Negev as far as Bethel, to the place where his tent had been at the beginning, between Bethel and Ai, to the place of the altar which he had made there formerly; and there Abram called on the name of the LORD.
>
> (13:1–4)

What do you think Abram said to the LORD at the altar of Bethel? "Lord, look at what a faithful servant I have been"? Not a chance! That killing stone must have been wet, both with Abram's tears and with the blood of an unblemished lamb—the atoning sacrifice for sin. Abram "called on the name of the LORD" that day as a convicted sinner. And as a sinner who knew that there was a sacrifice for sins!

Here again, we find that Abram is a bright example of faith—this time, faith, not simply in the promises of God, but also in the provision of God; faith in the God who justifies the ungodly! And we, failures though we are, must be people of the same faith. God makes wonderful promises for those who trust and obey. But even better news is that he has also made wonderful provision for those who haven't yet done so—not in a lamb from Abram's fold, but in the "Lamb of God who takes away the sin of the world" (John 1:29). Jesus has made provision for our forgiveness so that all of us who, with Abram, will "call on the name of the Lord will be saved" (Rom. 10:13).

FOR FURTHER STUDY

1. What does the New Testament have to say about Abram (Abraham)? How is he an example to us? How else is his faith commended? Who are to be considered his children?
2. Genesis 14:17–20 deals with a character named Melchizedek. Read Hebrews 7 for more information on this man. Who do you think he was? Why is he important?

TO THINK ABOUT AND DISCUSS

1. Abram treated his wife quite selfishly. What does the Bible say about how a man should treat his wife? And why is this important? (See Eph. 5:25–33.)
2. What is so commendable about Abram's actions in chapter 13? In what ways do they reflect the generosity of Jesus towards us? What are some of the specific, practical ways you can reflect Jesus' generosity towards the "Lots" in your life?

6 Abram believed God

(15:1–18:15)

Abram's story reminds us of a soap opera. In one episode we find him the triumphant man of faith, believing God for the birth of a miracle child, and we say to ourselves, "Abram believed God!" But in the following episode, we see him fathering an illegitimate child, squabbling with his wife, and in a whole heap of trouble. Now it is "Abram believed God?" that we find ourselves proclaiming!

Though he was a man of faith, Abram was sometimes as unpredictable as the wind. But the one constant in this story is God. Abram is known to us as a man of faith, not because his trust never wavered, but because God, the object of that trust, never wavered. God was the anchor to which Abram's fledgling boat was always attached. And thus (because of God's immovability), Abram's faith remained. Follow the story through chapters 15–18.

Abram believed God

In the middle of chapter 15, we find one of the most important sentences in the Old Testament: "Then he [Abram] believed in the LORD; and He [the LORD] reckoned it to him as righteousness" (15:6). God had come to Abram in a night vision (15:1) and promised him the unthinkable—a family. Now Abram and his wife, Sarai, were childless. They were also old—well beyond child-bearing age. But here God promised that Abram's heir would not be one of his servants, but a son of his own (15:4). And not only would Abram and Sarai have a son, but also God would bless that son so that, in years to come, the descendants of Abram would have family reunions of the largest proportions (15:5) and would possess the land of promise (15:18).

God had promised something quite impossible to Abram. Not improbable—impossible! Eighty-plus-year-old couples don't have babies! But here was God promising just that! Put yourself in Abram's shoes. Would you not wake up from your sleep, shake your head, and tell yourself you should not have eaten that chocolate before lying down? Not Abram. When faced with the unthinkable, we find that Abram simply "believed in the LORD."

Abram's unwavering faith is a striking example of how we, too, ought to trust God unwaveringly. For does he not make some seemingly impossible promises to us? "God causes *all things* to work together for good to those who love God" (Rom. 8:28)? Simply "Believe in the Lord Jesus, and you will be saved" (Acts 16:31)? "That's it?" we may ask. "Don't I have to join something, or give something, or promise something? Just believe in Jesus, and nothing more? That seems impossible." Impossible, but true! And Abram teaches us, by example, to simply take God at his word.

Now I say again that this verse contains one of the most important sentences in the Bible: "Then he [Abram] believed in the LORD; and He [the LORD] reckoned it to him as righteousness." Paul picks up on this theme and quotes this verse a couple of times in his New Testament epistles (see Rom. 4 and Gal. 3). And he does so, not only to demonstrate *that* we should believe, but also to show what happens *when* we believe in the Lord. In both places (Romans and Galatians), Paul emphasizes that, when Abram believed in the LORD, God "reckoned it to him as righteousness." In other words, Abram was brought into a right relationship with God on the basis of his belief—his faith, or trust.

This is crucial, because, when someone poses the question "How can we be made right with God?", the kinds of answers that often follow are things like: go to church, obey the Ten Commandments, read the Bible more often, and so on. But we need to notice something quite refreshing in Genesis 15:6. "How can we be made right with God?" Well, all Abram needed to do was to believe—to take God at his word. He didn't have to perform good works; he didn't have to make any promises. He simply had to trust what God had said, and he was reckoned as righteous in God's sight.

The same is true for us—so that Paul can summarize in Romans 3:28: "we maintain that a man is justified [reckoned righteous] *by faith* apart from works of the Law." How can *we* be reckoned as righteous? The same way Abram was: by faith; by believing what God tells us. And what does God tell *us*? "He made Him who knew no sin [Jesus] to be sin on our behalf, so that we might become the righteousness of God in Him" (2 Cor. 5:21). God sent Jesus to take our sins upon himself. And if we will simply take God at his word—if we will simply trust what Jesus has done for us—it will be reckoned to us as righteousness!

Abram believed God?

Now there is no doubt that Abram trusted the LORD. He was indeed a man of faith. But the sad tale of Genesis 16 reminds us that even the best of God's people are prone to fall prey to many foolish desires. Think it out. Abram and his wife, Sarai, had God's astonishing promise: "You will have a son." And though God had not specifically said, "You will have a son *by your wife*," that was clearly the implication—that is how men are supposed to have sons! So, clearly, Abram and Sarai had a promise together. And initially Abram, if not his wife Sarai, believed God.

But some time had passed between chapters 15 and 16, and they still had no son. Abram and Sarai weren't getting any younger. And Sarai began to get impatient. So impatient, in fact, that she started to "do God's thinking for him."[1] Sarai was desperate. God did not seem to be coming through, so she came up with a plan of her own (16:2). Maybe Hagar, her slave-girl, could act as a surrogate mother. "After all, she is just a slave," Sarai must have thought; "it will be no big deal to use *her* this way."

Observe Sarai. She was *bitter*, muttering to herself, "The LORD has prevented me from having children." She was *callous*, treating her slave-girl as something less than human.

And, worst of all, in her weird, warped world, Sarai was *wiser than God*! And Abram fell right in with her—and into bed with his cleaning lady! He doesn't seem like the man of faith now. He and his wife both lost sight, temporarily, of God's promises—and reaped a whirlwind of disappointment and dysfunction.

Now, in all this nonsense, Abram didn't lose his right standing with God. But he did suffer great heartache and misery because of his momentary lapse in judgment. His family would never be the same again. Because of the family dysfunction that began in chapter 16, Abram eventually lost his son Ishmael forever in chapter 21. And oh, how many people live with a lifetime of pain, difficulty, or heartache because somewhere along the line they thought they were wiser than God! God's Word was clear enough, but because of the heat of the moment, the influence of our friends, or our own lack of patience, we leapt into an incredibly foolish decision. Perhaps you've never thought of it this way. But so much of the tangled web you are now bemoaning may date directly back to "that night," "that summer," "that relationship," or "that season of life."

> How many people live with a lifetime of pain, difficulty, or heartache because somewhere along the line they thought they were wiser than God!

The pain is real. And the pain may last a lifetime. But "If we confess our sins, He is faithful and righteous to forgive us our sins and to cleanse us from all unrighteousness" (1 John 1:9). If we are people of faith—if we believe God's promises made in Christ—we do not have to carry our sins and sorrows to the grave!

What is faith?

In spite of Abram's folly, we can learn a great deal from him regarding faith. What is faith? What is it not? We have already begun to see some answers in Genesis 15–16, and we will see some more as we continue into chapters 17 and 18.

Faith is a response to God's Word

Faith was not Abram working up, in himself, some confidence that God was going to bless him. Regrettably, that is how faith is often portrayed in our day—a quality worked up in an individual who is "believing God" for a windfall of his or her own imagination. That is not what we see in the account of Abram (ch. 15). He didn't decide that, if he would just believe enough, God would give him a son. On the contrary, the whole thing was God's idea. Abram simply responded to the promise of God. Abram simply took God at his word. The lesson? If we desire more faith, we ought to get ourselves more familiar with God's Word! Faith is a response to God's Word!

Faith is not perfection

Abram proves in chapter 16 that a person can be a true believer and still really blow it! That is not to excuse our sin. But it is to say that our faith—and, ultimately, our salvation—rests not on our performance, but on God's promise. God is the object of our trust. And since he doesn't change, we may continue to trust him, even though we vacillate.

Faith never gives up

When Abram was seventy-five (12:1–3), God had promised to make him into a great nation, and to bless all the families of the earth through his descendants. But when chapter 17 opens, Abram is ninety-nine years old and has almost nothing to show for all the promises God had made—only a thirteen-year-old illegitimate son. Yet Abram trusted God for each of these twenty-four years! So, if you've been waiting for what seems like a long time for God to answer your prayers, here is hope from Genesis 17:1–8: God never forgets his people or his promises! "I *will* multiply you exceedingly" (v. 2); "you *will* be the father of a multitude of nations" (v. 4); "I *will* make you exceedingly fruitful" (v. 6); "kings *will* come forth from you" (v. 6). "I *will* do what I said I would do," says the LORD. Abram believed. And faith keeps believing even when God seems slow to deliver. Faith never gives up!

Faith is the gift of God

As excited as Abram was about the promise of a legitimate child by Sarai (17:15–16), he was still concerned for the welfare of his illegitimate son, Ishmael. He asked God, in fact, that the blessings promised to himself might extend to Ishmael (17:18). And God's response is as curious as it is firm: "I will bless him ... But My covenant I will establish with Isaac" (17:20–21). *God* decided that Isaac, and not Ishmael, would be the father of the chosen people—the descendants of Abram!

Clearly Isaac would later have to believe in God as his father had done. But verse 21 is a reminder that the reason why Isaac would later believe like his father was because God had chosen him! God designated Isaac as the father of the family of faith—before he was ever born! Isaac believed because God chose him for that very purpose! And that is a wonderful reminder that faith does not spring from the content of our own characters, from the wisdom of our own hearts, or even from the exercise of our own wills. Faith is "the gift of God" (Eph. 2:8)!

Faith results in change

In chapter 17, both Abram and Sarai had their names changed by God himself. Abram ("exalted father") became Abraham ("father of a multitude"). And Sarai became Sarah, which means "princess."[2] Why did God change their names? As a symbol of their changed status! Abraham was now living under God's covenant blessings. And Sarah was now God's princess, destined to be the mother of Israel! They had gone from barren to blessed. And, in the ancient context in which they lived, such a change called for brand new names.

Now, in most modern cultures, we do not change our names when we become believers in Jesus. But our status is no less changed than was Abraham's or Sarah's. We, too, have gone from barren to blessed. We have gone from being guilty to being innocent; from being God's enemies to being his friends; and, as we will see in the next section, from being disobedient sinners to being saints with the capacity and desire to obey God!

Faith is demonstrated by obedience

James the brother of Jesus made this point quite well when

he said that "faith, if it has no works, is dead" (James 32:17), and claimed, "I will show you my faith *by my works*" (James 2:18). Faith and works are not synonymous. But good works *are* the inevitable result of true faith. And Abraham illustrates this. In 17:9–14 God declared that the sign of his covenant with Abraham would be that Abraham should circumcise all the males in his house. Easy for us to say, since, in our modern, health-related practice of circumcision, we do the deed right at birth, leaving no memory of the pain. But Abraham, remember, was ninety-nine years old. His son was thirteen, and his servants were all grown men. To circumcise them all would not be an easy task. But this was what God asked. So Abraham faced a test. Would he really trust God, even when it was difficult? Would he prove his faith by obeying the God in whom he supposedly trusted? Yes, he would (17:23). Abraham did just "as God had said"! He demonstrated his faith by obedience. And so must we!

Abraham was a man of faith! He believed God when the promise seemed impossible. He believed God even when his wife laughed (18:1–15). He got back on track after a momentary lapse in judgment. And he demonstrated that he trusted God by practical obedience. May God give us grace to do the same!

FOR FURTHER STUDY

1. Read Romans 4 and Galatians 3. What conclusions does Paul draw from Abram's faith? How does he apply them to New Testament believers?
2. Genesis is filled with examples of God's choosing of individuals—Abram out of the land of the Chaldeans (ch. 12); Isaac over Ishmael (ch. 17); Jacob over Esau (ch. 25). Read Romans 9. What ongoing implications does Paul draw from these events? How does God's choosing relate to our salvation?
3. Read James 2—faith demonstrated by obedience. How can we put together James's strong language about works with Paul's strong language regarding faith (see Eph. 2:1–10; Rom. 3:21–4:25)?

TO THINK ABOUT AND DISCUSS

1. Have there been occasions when you, like Abram, have waited a very long time to see God fulfill his promise or answer a prayer? What did you learn during those years of waiting? Or are you still waiting? And what can you learn from observing Abram during the twenty-plus years between God's promise (ch. 12) and its fulfillment?
2. God chose Isaac as the child of the promise before he was even born. If you are a believer, think back to that time when you first came to believe in Christ. Looking back, can you discern how God was working to draw you to himself before you even realized it? What do these experiences teach us about grace?

7 Hellfire and brimstone

(18:16–20:18)

August 6, 1945 dawned like any other day. Men rode off on their bicycles to work. Housewives folded laundry and swept floors. Children bustled off to school. Young mothers dutifully changed dirty diapers and nursed their babes.

They could not have known that creeping towards their city like a hungry tiger was the *Enola Gay*, a United States bomber. They could not have known that it carried with it sure and instant death. But in the blink of an eye, the men with their bicycles and the women with their laundry were engulfed in white-hot flames. The schoolchildren and their teachers were incinerated in their classrooms. The mothers and their babies went into eternity together. And the city of Hiroshima had its name written in bold print in the annals of world history.

That was only a few decades ago. But we might well take what we know of Hiroshima and project it back into the account of Sodom. The story is much the same. "In the days of Lot," says Jesus, "they were eating, they were drinking, they were buying, they were selling, they were planting, they were building; but on the day that Lot went out from Sodom it rained fire and brimstone from heaven and destroyed them all" (Luke 17:28–29). No prophet to warn them. No message from an angel. The men, women, and children of Sodom and Gomorrah were caught completely off guard, to their everlasting destruction.

A tour of the city

Now it is easy to use Sodom and Gomorrah as a byword; to separate ourselves from them because "Of course they deserved to die. We know what God thinks about homosexuality." Yes, we do—he hates it. But we must be willing, also, to recognize that, though homosexuality was the sin that finally wore God's patience with Sodom threadbare, there were other sins in Sodom and Gomorrah! In fact, Genesis 19:32 informs us that there were not even ten righteous people in the whole place. And a look around the city reveals that many of these unrighteous persons looked a lot like the folk we interact with daily at the workplace, in the market, or at the school. In fact, they looked a lot like us!

So let's take a tour of the city, just hours before all its inhabitants were wiped off the map. What kind of people lived there? We might be surprised to see our own reflections in one or two of their faces—and, in so doing, we might be a little better prepared to meet our Maker.

Man of prayer

Let's actually start our tour outside the city walls on

overlooking hillside near the village of Mamre. That is where we will find Abraham, the man of prayer (18:16–33).

Before the destruction of Sodom, the LORD had paid a visit to Abraham's tent (18:1–5). As he was about to leave, he asked himself, "Shall I hide from Abraham what I am about to do?" (18:17). Then he turned and said to Abraham, "The outcry of Sodom and Gomorrah is indeed great, and their sin is exceedingly grave" (18:20). Why did the LORD give him warning? So there would be a witness to testify that it was God who destroyed the cities? To see how Abraham would respond to the destruction of his near neighbors? Both explanations seem possible—especially the latter.

Abraham had just put his wife in a position of extreme compromise (and was about to do it again in ch. 20). He had begotten an illegitimate child by his wife's servant girl. And he had treated that servant girl quite poorly afterward. In a very real sense, Abraham was just as guilty as Sodom. Yet Abraham the sinner had been forgiven by God again and again! How would he respond to the news of the impending destruction of his neighbors?

Well, in 18:22–33, we find that he pled that God might spare the city. Yes, he pled, primarily, on behalf of the righteous (18:23). But his plea was that God spare the entire city, homosexuals and all! What an example to some in our day who are so vindictive towards present-day Sodomites—using them for political target practice and proudly proclaiming, regarding the AIDS virus, that "they are getting what they deserve"! That may be so. But do we pause like Abraham to plead for their souls before our Redeemer? Do we recall that we also, like Abraham, are guilty sinners? Have we forgotten how much mercy the Lord has shown to us in Jesus?

How good it would be if we could see our reflection in the face of Abraham, the man of prayer! But let's continue our tour. We may see ourselves again in the city ...

Saved, but barely

Follow me down the hillside and across the valley to the gates of Sodom, where sits Abraham's nephew Lot (19:1). Lot had probably grown to believe in the LORD through his uncle Abraham. So he was a little bit of an oddity in Sodom—different enough, in fact, to have compassion on strangers who were prepared to spend the night on the streets (19:2–3). But he had also been assimilated quite well into this city of sin. He even had a seat at the city gate! To sit there, he must have been an elder in the city. And to have been an elder, he must have made some compromises with the lifestyle and morality of the city. So there he sits—an apparent believer, yet able to join the crowd and immerse himself in the culture of sin.

Lot was a man confused—torn between his upbringing in the faith and his enjoyment of the world.[1] So confused, in fact, that when the men of the city were at the door, prepared to gang-rape his guests, he offered them his daughters instead (19:4–8). Do you see the torment in his soul? He was desperate to protect his guests, as the LORD would want. But he was also desperate to make peace with the sinful culture in which he lived. So desperate, in fact, that he was willing to sell his daughters in the process (no wonder they learned to use sex to preserve themselves, 19:30–38).

Now, many a churchgoer may see his or her reflection in the tormented face of Lot. Some of us are torn. When God calls us to go forward with him, we hesitate like Lot (19:16). The opportunity for dishonest gain pulls at us powerfully. The temptation of sexual sin has laid down roots in our lives. Our friends, business partners, and neighbors are like the men of Sodom; and we, like Lot, are so often desperate to make a good impression with them and are willing to compromise to do so.

Lot was saved in the end, but barely. God had to drag him, by the collar, to safety. Perhaps, in his mercy, he will do the same with some of us. But why take the chance? Why do we not simply resign our positions as elders in Sodom now? Why not put our hands firmly into that of the Savior today?

Haters of God

Step outside Lot's door now and observe the mob in the street (19:4–9). They are violent and angry; filled with homosexual lust; prepared to rape and even murder. And, even after being struck blind by God, they are still desperately trying to continue in their sin (19:11)! These men are not torn like Lot. They are, rather, tearing down his door to get what they want!

God forbid that we should see our faces reflected in this mirror. But could it be that someone who has picked up this little book has sunk this low? Perhaps God has even laid you on a sick-bed or hamstrung you so that you can't keep up your sinful routine. Yet you have struggled all the more against him. You're a bit angry with God. You're not even sure, in fact, why you are reading this book! Perhaps it is simply that you might see yourself in the mirror of Genesis 19; that you might see that sin is suicidal; and that you might flee to safety in Jesus who died in your place!

Deaf to God's warning

Continuing our tour of Sodom, fast-forward with me to the following morning. Inside Lot's compound, all is in a frenzy. Lot and his wife are packing clothing, locating heirlooms, saddling their donkeys … and desperately trying to track down the two young men who are engaged to Lot's daughters. "Up, get out of this place," Lot says to them in 19:14, "for the LORD will destroy the city!"

But look at their faces. They smile knowingly. Lot appears to them "to be jesting"! They don't believe him, and why would they? Nothing in this man's life would make them view him as a faithful spiritual guide. They probably think of him as just another religious hypocrite who changes his clothes and his behavior one day in seven, then returns to his normal self the rest of the week. You can almost hear them laughing, "The old boy's gone mad! Go sober up, pops! You've had another long night."

Theirs is a popular line of thought. "These religious folk are all mad. They don't even practice what they preach." That was certainly true of Lot. But whether it is true of your local church or not does not invalidate the message.

> Lot's sons-in-law would tell us that the line "Church folk are all hypocrites" will not be a sufficient excuse when we stand before God's judgment seat.

Lot's sons-in-law would tell us that the line "Church folk are all hypocrites" will not be a sufficient excuse when we stand before God's judgment seat. They would tell us that the man at the front of the chapel, frantically warning people to flee the wrath to come, is not jesting; nor is he out of touch with reality. They would have sober words for the thousands who hear the message of salvation week after week but who are yet unsaved: "Please, stop turning a deaf ear to the gospel!"

Attached to the world

Finally, walk back with me to Lot's house and observe his wife, packing her belongings. She looks around longingly at her beautiful living room, a symbol of the status she has gained as a high-society woman in Sodom. She wishes she could take it all. Tears fill her eyes. She wonders whether or not she really wants to leave it all and follow God. And when it's time to go, the angels literally have to drag her, aching over the loss of everything that she holds dear, out of her home (19:16). That is why she "looked back" in 19:26. Because she, like the rich young ruler after her, loved her material possessions and her societal position more than she loved the LORD.

Maybe Lot's wife is the most modern of all the characters in the account. Her life, it seemed, consisted in the abundance of her possessions. Is that true of us? If someone were to ask us, "What are your chief ambitions in life?", would our answers be given in terms of job status, pay scale, and retirement possibilities? Would we speak of the dream house we've always wanted to build, the vacation we've always wanted to take, the financial security we hope to achieve, or the popularity we hope to attain? If so, there is a good chance that, when God calls us out of this world, we will find ourselves looking back … and left out of the kingdom. For Jesus says, "Remember Lot's wife. Whoever seeks to keep his life will lose it, and whoever loses his life will preserve it" (Luke 17:32–33).

Does it seem impossible that such a choice should ever have to be made in the English-speaking world—between comfort and Christ; between social acceptability and Christ; between job security and Christ? Some who read these pages will likely live long enough to see the day when Westerners (yes, Westerners) will be forced to choose between Christ and political freedom; between Christ and financial opportunity; between Christ and social acceptance; between Christ and our very lives. And if we find ourselves looking back now, what will happen to us then?

"No one," says Jesus, "after putting his hand to the plow and looking back, is fit for the kingdom of God" (Luke 9:62). Where is your treasure? Is it hidden with God in Christ? Or is it hanging on your wall, nestling in your bank account, or parked in your garage?

Flee the wrath to come

Finally, let us remind ourselves of what Jesus said in that famous reference to Sodom and Gomorrah to which we referred in opening this chapter: As it was "in the days of Lot," so it will be "on the day that the Son of Man is revealed" (Luke 17:28–30). Hellfire and brimstone will come again. Only, on that day, there will be no mountains and no town "near enough to flee to" (Gen. 19:20). Our only refuge will be in the shadow of the Lord Jesus, who alone can forgive the sins that bring God's judgment on the world. So why sit in the gates of Sodom any longer? Why wait another day to find rest and refuge in Jesus? "Behold, now is 'the acceptable time,' behold, now is 'the day of salvation'" (2 Cor. 6:2)!

FOR FURTHER STUDY

1. Do a study of the word "Sodom" in Scripture (using a concordance or online tool). How is the city referred to in the rest of Scripture? What lessons from Sodom are applicable for today?
2. The New Testament speaks of a different kind of people who are "saved, but barely"; not because of their love of the world, but because of their understanding of the gospel. Read 1 Corinthians 3:10–15. What does this say about: what we should look for in a church? how we should share the good news of Jesus with our neighbors? What kinds of modern religious trappings might be considered "wood, hay, straw"?

TO THINK ABOUT AND DISCUSS

1. What does the Bible say about homosexuality? How would you talk through these realities with a homosexual friend or co-worker? How could you identify with them in the gospel rather than condemning them? See Romans 1:18–32.
2. Notice how Lot (19:8), his daughters (19:30–38), and Abraham (20:1–13) all used sex to protect themselves and/or promote their agendas. How is sex used in our day (perhaps less obviously) for the same purposes (in innuendo, attire, advertising, etc.)? Are you using, or being used by, sex in these ways?

8 Promise and provision

(21:1–23:20)

Dinner was warm. The house was tidy. The table was set. And there we sat in the living room, waiting for our guest to arrive. But she never came.

Isn't it disappointing when people do not keep their word? We've all had it happen to us at one time or another. And when it does, we can become jaded and bitter; or develop a great fear of entrusting ourselves to other people; or take the attitude that, "If you want something done, you have to do it yourself." Worst of all, for many of us, these attitudes begin to color the way that we relate to God. Maybe we can't be sure if he will keep his word. We fear making too radical a commitment, lest we end up being hurt in the end. And we take matters into our own hands.

As he had promised

Do you have trouble taking God at his word? Then you need to hear the opening lines of Genesis 21:1–2: "Then the LORD took note of Sarah *as He had said*, and the LORD did for Sarah *as He had promised*. So Sarah conceived and bore a son to Abraham in his old age, at the appointed time *of which God had spoken* to him." Isn't that good to hear? It had been a long time coming, but God had not forgotten his promise to Sarah (17:19). God always does what he says he will do. He is not like us, forgetting, overlooking, and ignoring his commitments. Nor is he, like us, sometimes willing to fulfill his commitments, but unable to do so. He never runs out of time. He never gets sick, or has an unexpected scheduling conflict. And he never lacks the strength to do what he says he will do—even if the task is as tall as giving a baby to a ninety-year-old woman or raising his Son from the dead! Nothing is too hard for the Lord! And the Lord always does "as He had said."

Now read on into 21:3–4 and you will find that God wasn't the only one doing "as He had said"—so was Abraham! In verse 3, he named his new son Isaac, just as the LORD had instructed him back in 17:19. And in verse 4 we read that "Abraham circumcised his son Isaac when he was eight days old, *as God had commanded him*" in 17:10!

As we read, it would be easy to say to ourselves, "Amen! I am so glad I am trusting in and waiting on the Lord!" But are we really doing that? And are we proving it by doing what he says? Do our checkbooks reveal that we believe that God's kingdom investment plan really works? Does our treatment of others show that we believe God when he says, "Vengeance is mine, I will repay" (Rom. 12:19)? Do our schedules demonstrate that we believe that the Lord "gives to His beloved even in his sleep" (Ps. 127:2)? Do the decisions we make show that we believe God will do "as He [has] said"? Or are we taking matters into our own hands?

Those who live life based only on worldly wisdom will rarely have the experience of Sarah in verses 6–7: "God has made laughter for me; everyone who hears will laugh with me … Who would have said to Abraham that Sarah would nurse children? Yet I have borne him a son in his old age." What a sign of spiritual health laughter can be! Not laughter at the contrived levity that we call comedy—but a laughter that says, with Sarah, "Ha! I can hardly believe how good God has been to me!" Do you ever laugh like that? If not, is it a sign that, perhaps, your successes are not results of the surprising grace of God but simply of the run-of-the-mill paybacks of worldly wisdom?

Sarah had once laughed *at* God—disbelieving his promise of a son. But now she laughed *with* God, because his goodness was almost too good to be true.

Sarah had once laughed *at* God—disbelieving his promise of a son. Then she had tried to fulfill the promise herself, and found only heartbreak. But now Sarah laughed *with* God, because his goodness was almost too good to be true—and not only because of her old age. God's goodness to Abraham and Sarah was also too good to be true because it was so undeserved! Even if we hadn't seen the continued sin of Abraham and the unbelief of Sarah in previous chapters, Genesis 21:9–12 would be enough to convince us that God was not good to them because they had been good to him. No, Abraham and Sarah were, again, being treated better than they deserved. Not only had Sarah devised her own worldly-wise plans to get a son through her servant girl, but also Abraham had gone along with those plans. But now we find Sarah wanting to kick that servant girl and her son (whom Sarah had arranged for) out of the house.

Isn't this amazing? Sarah, who had been shown such kindness by God, and who was rejoicing in God's good provision, now shows utter contempt for another human being—her husband's own son, no less. What a reminder to us that God was not good to Sarah because Sarah was good. God was good to Sarah because *God* is good! And the same is true of us. If God has been good to us, it is "not on the basis of deeds which we have done in righteousness, but according to His mercy" (Titus 3:5).

The test

By the time we come to chapter 22, many years have passed. Abraham and Sarah had finally settled in. Their days of wandering about and living in makeshift tents were over. Sarah had probably gotten their home decorated just the way she liked it. Perhaps Abraham had planted a little garden. The servants had learned the ins and outs of the surrounding hillsides, perfecting the seasonal routines of cattle-driving and shepherding. And best of all, there was Isaac. He was becoming a young man now. He had proven to be a faithful and obedient son. He was learning to worship the God of his father. His shoulders were broad and his face was becoming like that of a man. Everything seemed just right.

And now this? Now, after God had given them every

earthly blessing, comes this? "Take now your son, your only son, whom you love, Isaac, and go to the land of Moriah, and offer him there as a burnt offering on one of the mountains of which I will tell you" (22:2). "Why?" Abraham must have thought. "Why this? Why now? O LORD, anything but Isaac!"

The wrenching in Abraham's heart must have answered his own question. Why now? Why Isaac? Because God had given Abraham much. And, like us, Abraham must have been tempted to love God's good gifts more than he loved God himself. And God's crowning gift—Abraham's most prized possession—was his son, his only son, whom he loved, Isaac. And thus, the loss of Isaac would be the keenest test of Abraham's faith in and love towards God. Would he still love God if God took away his good gifts? Would he still follow God if God took away his son, his only son, whom he loved, Isaac? These are questions we must ask of ourselves: "Would I still love God if I were put in the shoes of an Ethiopian, making around one dollar a day? Would I still love him if he took my home, my three meals a day, my children, or my spouse?"

Perhaps you have walked through such trials—the death of a loved one, or the loss of a fortune—and found God faithful on the other side. But I want you to notice that Abraham didn't wake up one morning and find Isaac dead. As testing as that may have been, God didn't simply *take* Isaac from Abraham. God gave Abraham the option of whether or not to *give* Isaac up in obedience to the LORD. That's a much greater test. It's the kind of test that Ann Hasseltine's parents got when they received the following lines from their would-be son-in-law, Adoniram Judson, asking for Ann's hand in marriage:

> I have now to ask, whether you can consent to part with your daughter early next spring, to see her no more in this world; whether you can consent to her departure for a heathen land, and her subjection to the hardships and sufferings of a missionary life; whether you can consent to her exposure to the dangers of the ocean; to the fatal influence of the southern climate of India; to every kind of want and distress; to degradation, insult, persecution, and perhaps a violent death. Can you consent to all this, for the sake of him who left his heavenly home, and died for her and for you; for the sake of perishing immortal souls; for the sake of Zion, and the glory of God? Can you consent to all this, in hope of soon meeting your daughter in the world of glory, with a crown of righteousness, brightened by the acclamations of praise which shall redound to her Saviour from the heathens saved, through her means, from eternal woe and despair?[1]

What will I say if I get a letter like that someday? What will I do if God calls my son to go to Saudi Arabia with the gospel? What will I do if being faithful to Christ means losing my job, or forfeiting my health, or endangering my family? I don't know yet, and neither do you! That is why we need, so badly, to be tested.

So "Consider it all joy, my brethren, when you encounter various trials, knowing that the testing of your faith produces endurance. And let endurance have its perfect result, so that you may be perfect and complete, lacking in nothing" (James 1:2–4). Did you catch that? In order to be "complete" we must "encounter various trials." And before we do, let us learn from Abraham, and from his son.

Abraham believed God

Imagine the night that passed between 22:2–3. Abraham could not have slept a wink. Perhaps he tossed and turned. Perhaps he paced the floor—praying, crying, and pleading with the LORD. He may even have found himself questioning God. "I thought you said that You were going to make me 'the father of a multitude of nations' [17:4]. I thought you said that 'through Isaac [my] descendants shall be named' [21:12]. How can that be if I now have to sacrifice him? I don't understand."

Those are good questions. We'll find the answers to them in just a moment. But first, let's simply notice that Abraham did what God said. Did he have questions? Surely. Was his task difficult? More than any of us can know. But the difficulty of the task and the questions involved never provide us with an adequate reason to disobey or drag our feet when we have a clear command from God. "So Abraham rose early in the morning and saddled his donkey, and took two of his young men with him and Isaac his son; and he split wood for the burnt offering, and arose and went to the place of which God had told him" (22:3). That is true obedience: doing as God says, even when we don't have all the details—and even when God's instructions don't make sense. Is there a situation like that in your life right now?

Abraham, amazingly, obeyed God. But the question is, "Why?" Was he just morally good-natured? No. We've already seen what kind of a sinner he was. So how does a sinner like Abraham come to a place where he is able to obey God so steadfastly in such a difficult situation? By faith! By believing that God, not Abraham, knows best! And in this case, by believing that God would do what he said he would do. God had promised to make Abraham, through Isaac, a great nation. Abraham believed that. Thus, Abraham believed that somehow, in some way, God would spare Isaac's life through this ordeal. That is why, in 22:5, he told his servants to "Stay here with the donkey, and I and the lad will go over there; and we will worship *and return to you.*"

Abraham was not sugarcoating the situation. He was not lying. He really believed that he and the lad would both be back. He really believed that, because of God's promise concerning Isaac, God would somehow, in some way, preserve the boy's life. And Hebrews 11:17–19 tells us just what was going through his mind:

> By faith, Abraham, when he was tested, offered up Isaac, and he who had received the promises was offering up his only begotten son; it was he to whom it was said, "In Isaac your descendants shall be called." He considered that God is able to raise people even from the dead, from which he also received him back as a type.

Instead of disobeying God's instructions and doubting God's promises, Abraham was busy brainstorming how God might make it all work together for his good!

Isn't that astounding? God's instructions seemed to contradict God's character and God's promises. But, instead of disobeying God's instructions and doubting God's promises, Abraham was busy brainstorming how God might make it all work together for his good! And he came up with a possible solution—resurrection! "Perhaps that is what God is going to do," he thought. "After the sacrifice, God is going to raise Isaac from the dead—because God will not fail to keep his promise! Isaac *will* live!"

That is faith! Believing that God will work this seemingly impossible situation for my good so that I am able, in spite of my questions, to obey! And though God worked the situation out another way, as we will see, the lesson is still the same. Abraham believed God would do what he said he would do. And when hope seemed lost, Abraham thought deeper and deeper about the God he served until his hope was restored.

Do you have that kind of faith in God? When the going gets tough, do you have a mind that defaults, not to brainstorming your own solutions, but to brainstorming the miraculous ways God might work the situation out for your good and his glory? If you do, then you will have enough light at the end of the tunnel to keep going—and to do what God says!

Isaac's obedience

In putting ourselves exclusively into Abraham's shoes, we haven't stopped to think about how all this must have felt for Isaac. It must have seemed a bit strange when, in 22:5, Abraham left the servants behind. But Isaac picked up the pile of wood that one of them had been carrying, and hiked along. But something else was nagging at his young mind. They had all the ingredients for a sacrificial worship service—except the most important: the offering itself. So Isaac asked his dad in verse 7, "... where is the lamb for the burnt offering?" and got this cryptic reply: "God will provide for himself the lamb for the burnt offering, my son."

Now, some of us might have found ourselves asking, "What do you mean, Dad? Do you expect that God is just going to make a lamb appear out of thin air? Don't you think that, if God were going to provide the lamb, he would have provided it by means of us bringing it with us when we left home this morning?" We wouldn't fault Isaac for being confused at this point, and perhaps even a bit frustrated at his dad's nondescript replies.

But, if Isaac thought those kinds of thoughts, he didn't say them. All we read in verse 8 is that "the two of them walked on together." Perhaps he had seen his father trust God for provision in the past. Maybe he had even heard these same words from his father's lips many times growing up: "God will provide, my son." And he had surely seen God do it! You see, young Isaacs do not come out of nowhere. They come from parents whom they observe obeying the Lord even when it is tough. They come from parents who believe—and live as though they believe—that the Lord will provide! And look how children like that turn out: "Then they came to the place of which God had told him; and Abraham built the altar there and arranged the wood, and bound his son Isaac and laid him on the altar, on top of the wood" (22:9).

Now verse 6 becomes really important. In verse 6 we read that Isaac, not Abraham, carried the wood. Isaac must have been very close to full grown at this point—strong enough to do the heavy lifting in place of his aging father. In other words: stronger than his father. This was no chubby toddler Abraham was tying to the stake here. This was a big, strapping teenager—the kind that, though Dad doesn't like to admit it, could now whip his father in a wrestling match. And Abraham was well over a hundred years old. So now you get the picture of what was really happening here. Abraham was only able to tie Isaac down to the altar because Isaac was willing to be tied down! And why was Isaac willing? Because his father's faith in the God of the impossible had rubbed off on him. He believed what his father had said in verse 8: "God will provide for Himself the lamb for the burnt offering, my son." And if God chose him to be the lamb, then God knew best!

I say to you again: teenagers like that do not come out of nowhere. They do not generally arise out of families that are thoroughly moral but only marginally Christian. They arise out of families where Christ has come to have first place in everything!

God's provision

Let's hurry on to the climax of the account. Just as Abraham, hands trembling and forehead dripping with sweat, draws his killing knife in verse 10, the angel of the LORD speaks: "'Do not stretch out your hand against the lad, and do nothing to him; for now I know that you fear God, since you have not withheld your son, your only son, from Me.' Then Abraham raised his eyes and looked, and behold, behind him a ram caught in the thicket by its horns" (22:12–13).

Abraham had passed the test! He had laid aside his doubts and fears and done what God said—so that the angel could say, "now I know that you fear God." Did God know ahead of time what Abraham would do? Yes. The Bible teaches that God always knows the end from the beginning (see Ps. 139:4, 16; Prov. 19:21; Eph. 2:10). But Abraham had yet to prove his faith and love for God in time and space. And so, in that sense, God was *seeing* it for the first time, and, in that sense, could say, "*now* I know that you fear God." And, perhaps more importantly, *Abraham* was also seeing how strong his faith had become.

Do you know who else passed the test in these verses? God! At the opening of the chapter it seemed that God was forgetting all the promises he had made to Abraham. If we had lived at the beginning of Genesis 22, we might have given up on God. But not Abraham. Through his obedience, Abraham gave God a chance to prove himself. And God came through, just as he always comes through. So learn a lesson here. God's severe testings in your life are not merely meant to test and prove *your faith*, but also to give you a chance, through your obedience, to test and prove *his faithfulness*! And God always passes the test. There is always a ram in the thicket! And so Abraham named that mountain Jehoveh-Jireh, "The LORD Will Provide."

God's severe testings in your life are not merely meant to test and prove *your faith,* but also to give you a chance, through your obedience, to test and prove *his faithfulness*!

We see in the verses that follow that God continued to provide—to do "as He had promised." In verses 15–18, God reiterates his covenant promises to Abraham and Isaac. In verses 20–24, he anticipates the fulfilling of those promises with the announcement of the birth of Rebekah, who will become Isaac's wife and Israel's mother. In chapter 23, his pledge of the promised land begins to be fulfilled as Abraham procures a burial plot in the land of Canaan. And in 22:19, Abraham and Isaac return home, having had their faith both tested and proven, and having had God's promises tested, proven, and reaffirmed. And everyone lived happily ever after, right?

God will provide the lamb

Well, yes, Abraham, Sarah, and Isaac did live happily ever after. But if we closed the chapter there, we would have missed the most important lesson of the account: that there is more to this story than Abraham and Isaac. In point of fact, this story is one of the brightest, most colorful of all the Old Testament portraits of our Lord Jesus.

Like Isaac, Jesus faced a sacrificial death at the hands of his own Father. Like Isaac, Jesus took up the wood on which he would give his life and carried it into the countryside of Moriah, around what we now know as Jerusalem. Like Isaac, Jesus had questions about his Father's plan: "if you are willing, remove this cup from Me." But, like Isaac, Jesus faithfully obeyed his Father: "yet not My will, but Yours be done" (Luke 22:42).

But that is where the similarities end. For Jesus, there was no ram in the thicket. For Jesus, there was no substitute. Jesus' Father actually went through with what Abraham only contemplated: sacrificing his Son, his only Son, whom he loves—for the sake of sinners. Isaac was spared, but God "did not spare His own Son, but delivered Him over for us all" (Rom. 8:32).

Therein lies the reason why there was no substitute for Jesus. Jesus was acting as the substitute for "us all." There was no ram in the thicket for him because he himself was *our* ram in the thicket. And as Genesis 22:13 speaks of the ram's sacrifice for Isaac, so we may speak of Jesus' sacrifice for us: God "went and took the ram [Jesus] and offered him up ... in the place of" sinners.

We need to hear this because, in looking at Abraham's faith and obedience, we've set the bar quite high. Yet none of us, when tested, will pass with no marks against us. None of us obeys God fully as we ought. None of us trusts God in everything. We all find ourselves doubting, questioning, finagling, doing God's thinking for him, and many times disobeying his clear commandments outright. And even if we, like Abraham, grew to a place of maturity where we *did* pass the test, we would not be able to blow away the foul stench of our past! For all Abraham's victory in chapter 22, he could not erase the selling of his wife in chapters 12 and 20, nor his adultery in chapter 16!

It doesn't matter how much perfume you pour into a septic tank, you cannot get rid of the odor. And so it is with our sins. No matter how much good we do, we cannot erase the bad we have done. And no matter how much good we do today, we cannot tell how we may falter tomorrow. So we should, apart from faith in Christ, picture ourselves in the place of Isaac in verse 10: God's knife poised above us, ready to come down on our throats as a just penalty for our sins against his holiness and justice.

We need a Savior! We need a substitute. We need a ram, caught in God's thicket, which will willingly lie down on the altar and bleed in our place. And that is what we have in Jesus—"the Lamb of God who takes away the sin of the world" (John 1:29). But we can only have him if we, like Abraham, trust that "God will provide the lamb." We can only have him if we, like Abraham, stop trying to create our own solutions and submit ourselves to God's. Have you done that? If not, then, in Genesis 22, behold "the Lamb of God who takes away the sin of the world"—and believe!

FOR FURTHER STUDY

1. Think back through the life of Abraham (chapters 12–23) and compile a list of "Facts about faith" based on his example. For instance: "Faith is demonstrated by obedience" (17:9–14); "Faith is rewarded with provision" (22:10–14).
2. Think back through the life of Abraham and compile a list of the ways God kept his promises to him. Before you start, look carefully at 12:1–3 and notice all the facets of God's promises.

TO THINK ABOUT AND DISCUSS

1. Has God been asking you to do something that does not seem to make sense? What is it? Search to see if there are specific Bible promises that relate to your situation. Brainstorm (like Abraham) with a trusted Christian friend the ways in which God might be working a blessing.
2. When was the last time you "laughed" (though not necessarily outwardly) at the provision of God, or the last time you were surprised and overjoyed by grace? Is this a normal experience for you? Or do most of your provisions seem to come only as a result of your efforts?

Part 3
Isaac and Jacob—men of God's own choosing

(24:1–36:43)

9 All in the family

(24:1–26:35)

Genesis 24 contains one of the most beautiful stories in the Bible—a love story, with all the elements that would make a charming screenplay.

Young Isaac Abramson, devastated by the loss of his mother, wanders without comfort through the lonely corridors of his life. But one day, at the arrangement of his wealthy and devoted father, and through the wooing of a faithful family servant, a caravan arrives from the countryside, and into Isaac's life steps a bright, modest, beautiful young woman. A lonely young nobleman ... a devoted father ... a dedicated servant ... a well-bred bride—*a match made in heaven!*

What a film it might make! But as we let the story of Isaac and Rebekah play in the theatres of our minds, I want you to see that this account was made for something much more important than television. This account was written, and recorded in Holy Scripture, for our spiritual instruction and edification.

Imitate their faith

One of the things that makes this such an intriguing story is the faith and character displayed by the various people involved. Let's sketch them in briefly.

Abraham the devoted father

Abraham was passionately concerned about Isaac's future—specifically, that Isaac not take a wife "from the daughters of the Canaanites" (24:3) but from his own relatives (24:4). Why? The Canaanites were idol worshippers. And a Canaanite wife might well lead his son or his grandchildren astray. And more than anything else, Abraham wanted his family to remain faithful to the LORD. In that sense, Abraham is a model for every believing parent. Every Christian parent ought to want—more than fortune, fame, or education—their children to walk with the Lord. And that means that every Christian parent ought to be intimately and helpfully involved, as their children mature, in helping them choose wisely in matters of education, career, and certainly marriage.

Eliezer the praying servant

We learned in chapter 15 that Abraham's servant was called Eliezer. Here in chapter 24 we find him assigned a difficult task: travel a few hundred miles (without either the father or the groom) and pick a suitable wife for Isaac! What if he made a foolish choice? He simply couldn't do *that*. The task was too important. So what did Eliezer do? He prayed! Listen to him in verse 12: "O LORD ... please grant me success." And notice that, not only did he pray, but he prayed *specifically*—he asked God for a sign (24:13–14). And not just any sign, but a sign that accorded with biblical principles. He asked God, through the sign, to guide him to a woman of character—one who had a servant's heart. And Eliezer is an example of how Christians should seek the Lord's guidance in every endeavor. First, we must pray. Next, we must pray for *specific* guidance. And third, we must pray for guidance that clearly matches up with what we already know from Scripture.

Rebekah the honorable young woman

Rebekah is an example of what every young woman ought to be. She was chaste (24:16). She had a servant spirit (24:18–19). She was hospitable (24:25). And she was modest (24:65). Rebekah was everything that modern teenage girls are so often encouraged *not* to be. Instead of locking herself in her room, she was out collecting water for her family. Instead of being glued to her cellphone, she was on the lookout for strangers who needed a drink. Instead of showing off her undergarments (or lack thereof!), Rebekah "took her veil and covered herself" as she prepared to meet her fiancé. And (wonder of wonders!) Isaac was attracted to her! Need we say more? Rebekah is a picture-perfect example for young ladies!

Behind the scenes

Now, this is a story that not only shows us how to act, but also teaches us how to think—about God. God was the one working behind the scenes to bring these two young people and their families together. So what do we learn about him in this love story? We learn that he is ...

A God who is faithful to all his promises

As he sent Eliezer out to find a bride, Abraham called God the "LORD ... who spoke to me and who swore to me" (24:7). He was remembering how God had promised him a family (ch. 12), specifically, a son (ch. 17); how he had given him that son (ch. 21); and how he had spared the boy's life (ch. 22). And he was reasoning to himself, and with Eliezer, that if God had been so faithful to his promises thus far, surely he would provide a wife to keep the promised family tree going! God always does exactly what he says he will do. Therefore, we, like Abraham, can trust him!

A God who knows what we need before we ask him

This is what Jesus said in Matthew 6:8. And this is what Eliezer discovered in verse 15: "Before he had finished speaking, behold, Rebekah ... came out with her jar on her shoulder." Why? Because God knew what Eliezer needed before he asked. So God began answering the prayer before he finished asking! Isn't that good to know? Whatever the decision or difficulty we may be facing, God already knows what we need. Our job is simply to ask him and believe!

A God who speaks clearly to those who seek him

One of the beauties of this story is how clearly God answered Eliezer's prayer—giving him exactly the sign he had requested so he could be sure of how to proceed. And that is how God deals with us. He may not always post neon signs that can be seen from miles away. But his Word is clear enough, isn't it? The Bible is not encoded with secret messages. Nor is it written on a scholarly plane that only the most educated can understand. There are difficult passages, to be sure. But, by and large, even a child can understand the basic teachings of the Bible if he or she is willing to listen. And even when the Bible doesn't provide black and white answers—on questions such as whom to marry, when to buy a house, or which job to take—the Lord finds a way to make his will clear for those who will earnestly and patiently seek him.

A God who is determined to save sinners

Here is, perhaps, the most important lesson of all from Genesis 24. The whole reason for this arranged marriage was to ensure that Abraham's family tree continued to grow—that the nation of Israel would assuredly come to birth. And why was that important? Because, as Jesus said in John 4:22, "salvation is from the Jews." God's plan of salvation for the whole world—Jews and Gentiles alike—depended upon a Jewish Messiah! And God is determined to save sinners. Therefore God was determined to send Jesus, the Messiah. And therefore God was determined to establish Israel, through which he would send this Messiah! So, way back in Genesis 24, God was so interested in saving you that he was orchestrating a marriage in the middle of nowhere to ensure that, in the fullness of time, you would have a Savior!

Like father, like son

As we continue on in the life of Isaac, there are more lessons to be learned from the family circle. In particular, we see that the apple usually doesn't fall very far from the tree. Abraham had two sons. We read (25:1–18) that, spiritually at least, Ishmael didn't look very like his dad. He was not the beneficiary of the LORD's covenant promises. And he did not demonstrate the generous character of his father. Instead, "he settled in defiance of all his relatives" (25:18). Isaac, on the other hand, was the spitting image of his father—which was sometimes a good thing, and sometimes not. Let's notice the family resemblance between Isaac and his father, Abraham, learning some lessons along the way.

Isaac inherited his father's sin nature

There was constant bickering in Abraham's family. Everyone knew that Isaac, and not Ishmael, was the favorite. So we are little surprised when we learn (25:19–34) that Isaac and Rebekah governed their home the same way—choosing favorites (25:28). At least, for Isaac's part, there is little doubt he learned this from his own parents! Like father, like son!

As we worked through Abraham's life in chapters 12–23, we saw his sin nature on display in various other ways, too. Probably the most memorable was his putting his wife in a position of compromise in order to protect his own back in chapter 12—and then his doing the same thing again in chapter 20! And here in 26:7–11, we remember that the apple doesn't fall far from the tree! Isaac passed his wife off as his sister and sold her to a foreign king to protect his own back. And he probably didn't think up this cowardly solution on his own. Though he had not been born when his father had pulled the same stunt, he had probably heard tell of it. And now, when put in a pinch, he resorted to the same tactics as his dad in order to save his own neck—like father, like son!

The lesson here is that, as parents, we can pass down horrible habits of sin to our children. Not only do they inherit a sin nature from Mom and Dad, but they often also pick up, by dint of their environment, their parents' specific sin habits. And while we magnify the fact that Jesus can redeem children from the "futile way of life inherited from [their] forefathers" (1 Peter 1:18), we do not minimize the fact that sin patterns often pass through the generations—particularly as children grow up and have families of their own. So there is strong caution in the tale of Abraham and Isaac.

Isaac inherited his father's promises

Abraham was the recipient of some amazing promises from the LORD (ch. 12): "I will make you a great nation"; "in you all the families of the earth will be blessed"; and "To your descendants I will give this land." And, as we discover in 26:1–6, God's intention all along was to pass those promises along to, and bring them to fulfillment through, Isaac. In 26:12–22, in fact, we see Isaac beginning to lay hold of some of the land that was promised to his father. Like father, like son.

Isaac imitated his father's faith

Yes, Abraham passed down his sin patterns to his son. But Abraham was a believer. Wherever Abraham went, he built an altar and called upon the name of the LORD (see 12:7, 8; 13:4, 18; 22:9). And each time he did so was a reminder to himself, and to his God, that he needed forgiveness. He needed a blood sacrifice that would atone for his sins. And he called on the LORD to forgive him. And so it is no surprise that we find Isaac, having grown up with a father like that, doing the same thing in 26:23–25. Isaac had learned from his dad what it was to sin. But he had also learned from his dad what it was to go to the LORD in faith, seeking and finding forgiveness for sin and rest for his conscience. Like father, like son.

Now, from these last two points, we learn an opposite lesson from the previous one. Not only can our sin habits be imbibed by our children, but so can the blessings of spiritual life! Salvationisnotinherited,infallibly, the way the covenant blessings of Abraham were inherited by Isaac. Salvation happens as each individual places his or her faith in the Savior. That's why we say that Isaac "imitated" rather than "inherited" his father's faith. But, though eternal salvation is not inherited genetically, the blessings of abundant life in Christ, as they are observed up close for eighteen years, can be a powerful testimony that pulls our children into the same manner of life, that urges them to imitate our faith. Growing up in a believing home (and one where that faith is obvious) is a tremendous blessing to a child.

The blessings of abundant life in Christ, as they are observed up close for eighteen years, can be a powerful testimony that pulls our children into the same manner of life, that urges them to imitate our faith.

So are our children learning, from us, that there is

happiness and blessing in following the Lord? Yes, we know they are learning what it is to sin (even from the best of parents). But are they learning, from Mom and Dad, what it is to go to the Lord in faith, seeking and finding forgiveness for their sins and rest for their souls?

FOR FURTHER STUDY

1. Do some research on biblical parenting (Deut. 6; Eph. 6; Proverbs, etc.). What sorts of commands are given to parents? As either parent or child, how, practically, have you seen these commandments work for your family's good? If you are a parent, how, practically, might you implement what you have left undone?
2. Read 1 Peter 3:1–6. How can your local church help young women develop the kind of character that Rebekah had? In your local context, what specific issues and temptations for young girls need particular prayer and attention?

TO THINK ABOUT AND DISCUSS

1. Is there an area in which you, like Eliezer, are in need of specific guidance? What are some specific biblical markers you could be requesting of God and looking for?
2. If you are a parent, are there personal sin patterns that you see reflected in your children? What are they? What, practically, can you do to help break the cycle? How do your answers connect with the gospel (1 Peter 1:18–19)?
3. Genesis 24 presents a preparation for marriage that is very different from what is common in the Western world. What lessons can be gleaned from the health of this story and applied to courtship today? What are the particular temptations that are present in our modern system of finding a spouse?

10 *Jacob* I loved?

(27:1–31:55)

Have you ever known someone who was just a dirty, rotten scoundrel, but who nevertheless seemed always to have everything go his or her way? Maybe there was someone with whom you worked or went to school whose character was arrogant, selfish, and dishonest, but who seemed to have been born with a silver spoon in his or her mouth. Perhaps you can picture that person in your mind's eye even now. If you can, you have a good idea of how the folk in Isaac's neighborhood probably thought of his son Jacob.

Jacob was a despicable character—a conniving, cheating, stealing lecher. Yet everything seemed to go his way. Jacob's story is one long litany of self-centeredness, deceit—and success. And as we read it, in the back of our minds, we need to ask the question: "Why?"

Why was such a rotten character blessed so profusely? In the process, we might just learn a little bit about ourselves and about our God.

So let's notice the different hats Jacob wore in his sordid career:

Jacob the con man

Jacob's scheming actually began in Genesis 25:31. He took advantage of his brother's foolishness and stole his birthright. Jacob was an opportunist, not unlike those who run the lotteries, casinos, and pawn shops of our day. He had no scruples about taking advantage of someone's foolishness or desperation and sucking the life out of him or her.

But Jacob was not only an opportunist. He was also aggressive in his greed. Look at him in chapter 27, pulling the wool over his father's failing eyes. Look at him, particularly, in verses 18–25, willing to go to unbelievable lengths to make his lies work. And look at him in verse 20, willing even to take the name of the LORD on his lips to make his lies sound feasible. What a dastardly character! But he was not unlike many even in the churches of our day. Here is a young person hiding the truth from her parents. There is a fellow selling his car but not telling the whole truth about its collision history. Here is a businessman, working in a highly religious region and becoming tied to the local church because "it's good business." There is no shortage of Jacobs in our day. And they are no less repugnant.

Jacob the family man?

Chapter 29 opens with the promise of another beautiful love

story. Jacob was so in love with Rachel that he was willing to work seven years to earn her hand in marriage (29:18). But he soon found that Laban was up to no good. Laban deceived Jacob and gave him Leah instead. Laban's was a dirty trick, and his, we soon discover, was a dysfunctional family. But Jacob proved he fit right in. For it was not long until he and his wife were bickering (30:1–2); until he was falling into bed with his housemaids (30:3–13); and until Rachel and Leah were at each other's throats and bartering for sex (30:14–24).

Jacob's family was one giant mess! Pride, greed, deceit, jealousy, sexual immorality, and spite—sounds a lot like the modern family, doesn't it? But do you know which sin is most heinous of all in this story? Do you know which sin opened the floodgates for all the others? The fact that—except when God was giving them what they wanted—Jacob, Laban, Leah, and Rachel never spoke of him. Re-read chapters 29–30 and you will find that it is true. The only thing God seemed to be good for was to meet their own selfish desires. And maybe that is a sin we can relate to, as well. Some of us only pray when we're in trouble. Some of us only pray for ourselves. Some of us only obey because we want God to do something for us. And some of us only praise God when he does what we want. That was the sin that tore apart Jacob's family.

Jacob the businessman

Re-read 30:25–36. Does this sound like a healthy conversation between a man and his son-in-law? Their relationship seems to have been one strictly of business.

And it seems that Jacob viewed his whole life this way. Notice how, in verse 26, he thought of his wives and children as his wages. He called them "my wives and my children for whom I have served you"—almost as if he viewed them as his weekly paycheck. Notice also Jacob's self-reliance in verses 29–30: "But he said to him, 'You yourself know how I have served you and how your cattle have fared *with me*. For you had little *before I came* and it has increased to a multitude, and the LORD has blessed you *wherever I turned*.'" Jacob gave a little doff of the cap to the LORD's provision. But he was primarily giving himself the credit for his and Laban's financial success. He viewed everything as a business, with himself as the CEO.

How easy it is to view our families this way; to view our churches this way; to view our whole lives this way—using and commanding people so that we can have *our* goals achieved, and then becoming frustrated and indignant when others don't do what we want them to do. This is an especial danger, it seems, for fathers and church leaders—viewing our wives, our children, our members as little assets meant to build our empires. So get a good look at how ugly it was in Jacob's life and resign your position as self-appointed CEO!

How easy it is to view our families and churches this way—using and commanding people so that we can have *our* goals achieved.

Now, not only was Jacob a businessman, he was also a shady businessman, as we see in 30:27–43. Let's not stumble over Jacob's superstitious genetic-research project. The Bible is not teaching that Jacob's superstition had any scientific validity; only that Jacob thought it did—and that God supernaturally allowed Jacob's scheme to work (31:12). This paragraph is not teaching biology but the ways of providence—how God can, and sometimes does, work outside the norms of science. And what is important here is not the biology but the psychology. The important question is: Why did Jacob devise this scheme to begin with? The answer: To gain the upper hand over his father-in-law. This is an ancient example of a get-rich-quick scheme. And, like many modern get-rich-quick schemes, Jacob's plan had its roots in selfishness and dishonesty. Remember, Jacob was not only a businessman, but also a con man.

Jacob the spin man

Jacob's prosperity created a rift between him and Laban; so great a rift that Jacob realized that he needed to move his family away from Laban. But observe the forked-tongue way he went about it in 31:1–32. The problem was not *that* Jacob fled from Laban—God had told him to do so in verse 3. Rather, the problem was *how* he left. Jacob could (and should) have just said to his family and to Laban, "God has told me to return to the land of my fathers—so we are leaving." But that isn't what he said. Instead, Jacob became a spin doctor. He went into an elaborate political monologue meant to convince his wives that it really was OK to leave. It sounds like a campaign-year television ad:

> Hard-working. Honest. Religious. These are the words people are using to describe Jake Isaacson. For twenty years

> he has faithfully served his constituency. But the record of Laban proves that he is not the man to lead us forward. Ten times he has voted to lower the minimum wage. His record is a long litany of dishonesty and unfulfilled promises. So this year, vote Isaacson!

Jacob's speech is filled with enough exaggeration, enough mudslinging, and enough self-promotion to fit in quite nicely in any political campaign. But how easy it is to take this tack to make ourselves look better in the office, in the schoolhouse, in the neighborhood, at the family gatherings, and even at the church fellowship. But listen to how repulsive Jacob sounds, and remember that bad-mouthing others to improve your own position is morally reprehensible in any era.

Jacob, God's man

So Jacob was a lying son, a stealing brother, a cheating husband, a selfish father, and a mud-slinging son-in-law. Not much to be impressed with. And that is what makes Genesis 28:10–22 so amazing. For there we read that the LORD had a few words for this morally repugnant character, Jacob:

> I am the LORD, the God of your father Abraham and the God of Isaac; the land on which you lie, I will give it to you and to your descendants. Your descendants will also be like the dust of the earth, and you will spread out to the west and to the east and to the north and to the south; and in you and in your descendants shall all the families of the earth be blessed. Behold, I am with you and will keep you wherever you go, and will bring you back to this land; for I will not leave you until I have done what I have promised you.
>
> (28:13–15)

What? That is not what we would have expected to hear! The incongruity seems even more obvious when we read a verse like Romans 9:13: "Jacob I loved, but Esau I hated." *Jacob* I loved? How can that be? How could God love *Jacob*?

Well, the first part of the answer lies in *God's sovereignty*. Remember, God chose Jacob as the child of the promise before he and Esau were ever born (25:23). And the apostle Paul argued from this that God has the right to choose (or not choose) any one of us for salvation before we are ever born (Rom. 9). Retelling the account of Jacob and Esau, Paul said,

> ... though the twins were not yet born and had not done anything good or bad, so that God's purpose according to His choice would stand, not because of works but because of Him who calls, it was said to her, "The older will serve the younger." Just as it is written, "Jacob I loved, but Esau I hated." What shall we say then? There is no injustice with God, is there? May it never be! For He says to Moses, "I will have mercy on whom I have mercy, and I will have compassion on whom I have compassion." So then it does not depend on the man who wills or the man who runs, but on God who has mercy.
>
> (Rom. 9:11–16)

In other words, God loved undeserving Jacob to demonstrate that God, as God, can love anyone he chooses! He is sovereign. And in the same way that God chose Jacob before he was ever born, so God chooses everyone who ever becomes a son or daughter of the covenant. And it works the same way with each of us who inherits the promise of salvation in Jesus. We do not come into the world looking for God. We are born like sheep, each one turning to his or her own way (Isa. 53:6). And if God had not sought *us* before we sought *him*, none of us would ever seek him. If God hadn't chosen us before we chose him, none of us would ever have chosen him.

If God had not sought *us* before we sought *him*, none of us would ever seek him.

This is the genius of the gospel. This is how salvation can be absolutely free. God did not choose us because of anything we have done or will do. This is the whole lesson of Jacob's life. Whether or not an individual or family belongs to God is ultimately God's decision. And thank God it is. Because if we are anything like Jacob and his sons—and we have seen that we are—then we do not want to depend on our own works or our own wills but on God who shows mercy!

This mention of the Savior reminds us of the second reason why God chose Jacob—to demonstrate *God's grace*! We may read this account and protest, "This isn't fair. It isn't fair that God should choose Jacob and not Esau. It isn't fair that God permitted Jacob's schemes to work." And we would be absolutely correct. It isn't fair. What would have been fair would have been for God to have sent Abraham, Isaac, and Jacob's whole family to hell. They were all, in some ways, fairly rotten characters, as we have seen! And what would be fair would be for God to send all of us to hell, too. For there is a little bit of Jacob in each of us. Perhaps it comes out in different ways, but there is a con man in each of us; a spin doctor in each of us; a cheater in each of us; a greedy heart in each of us. And "the wages of sin is death" (Rom. 6:23).

So it may seem unfair that God loved Jacob, the scoundrel.

But you see, when we are thinking clearly, we really don't want God to treat us fairly. Rather, we want God to grant us his grace as he did Jacob! And thank God he has! He has given "His only begotten Son, [so] that whoever believes in Him shall not perish, but have eternal life" (John 3:16). Have you believed in the Son of God? Have you entrusted yourself to the God whose grace is given to us unfairly? If you have, then you realize that you and I are the dirty, rotten, undeserving scoundrels with the silver spoons in our mouths. Thank God!

FOR FURTHER STUDY

1. Use a concordance to look up the various other Bible passages that mention either Jacob or Esau. What else can we learn about them? How does God's choice of Jacob relate to us? What are we to learn from their examples?
2. Skim through the Genesis records in your mind. Are there other examples of God choosing one sibling over another in this book? What are the reasons given in each case? How do these examples tie in with what we learned about God's choice of Jacob?

TO THINK ABOUT AND DISCUSS

1. What was your first reaction when someone told you that God chooses whom he will save? What are the other alternatives? How does God's sovereign election fit together with human will?
2. Think through the sins of Jacob again. Is there anywhere you see your own face reflected in his poor example? Confess this to a friend and pray together for God's help (James 5:16).

11 A new name

(32:1–36:43)

Some time ago, some friends of mine traveled to Siberia to finalize the adoption of a little Russian boy. The process had dragged on for well over a year, during which time they had filled out hundreds of pages of paperwork, made two trips to Russia, spent thousands of dollars, shed many tears, and prayed every day … until, finally, we received a short email that began like this: "Well, it's official! We are now three. Aleksandr Aleksandrovich Mechev is now Edmond Aleksandr Huffman."

Why do you suppose they began their email that way? Why not simply say, "The adoption went through" or "Edmond is ours"? Why make their friends attempt to pronounce all those names? Because names are important; and because the changing of a name is especially important! In this case, little Edmond's new name symbolized that he had new parents, a new home, a new family, and a brighter future.

A new name is almost always the symbol of a new beginning. This is why adoptive parents are so excited when they finally have the adoption certificate; and why young women excitedly practice writing their fiancé's last name over and over. A new name symbolizes a new life! And this is what we see in Genesis 32–36. In these pages, Jacob, the deceiver, meets God, the Redeemer—and his life is completely and irreversibly changed. And, as a symbol of his new life—and of his adoption into God's family—Jacob gets a new name: Israel (32:28).

Now remember, Jacob was chosen by God before he was born (25:23). But God still needed to bring Jacob to a place in time when he would encounter God and be radically changed from the inside out. And the same is true for us. If you are saved, it is because you, like Jacob, were "chosen according to the foreknowledge of God the Father" (1 Peter 1:1–2). But none of us was born a Christian or a lover of God. Therefore, each of us needs to encounter God in such a way that our whole life is changed. Though we may not change our names, each one of us needs to be converted as Jacob was. For some of us, this has already happened; and for some of us, it still needs to. And Jacob's encounter with God in these chapters might just serve as a paradigm for how God has already met us, or might someday do so.

The crisis

The turnaround in Jacob's life began with a crisis (32:1–21). In front of him was Esau, who, for all he knew, was on a mission of revenge. And behind him was Laban, who was also none too pleased with Jacob. If he went forward, Jacob was marching into a potential minefield. But, because of the bridges he had burned between himself and Laban, he could not retreat. So he was stuck. He was afraid (32:7). And, in verses 9–12, he did what many of us do when we are stuck and afraid—he prayed.

How kind of the LORD to drop Jacob into the middle of a crisis so that, finally, he would turn his attention to the LORD! The jam Jacob was in was all of his own making. But God used it to allow Jacob to see how foolish he had been and how much he had offended him. What a mercy times of crisis can be! Perhaps you have witnessed how sickness, the loss of a loved one, a national emergency, or a public embarrassment can be used of God to humble our hearts and to call upon his name. Sometimes God's appointed means of grace is getting us stuck and afraid.

Sometimes God's appointed means of grace is getting us stuck and afraid.

Up until this point, Jacob had been prideful and arrogant (remember his speech in ch. 31?). But not until he was in trouble was he willing and able to say, "I am unworthy" (32:10). It is the specific conviction "*I* am unworthy," not a general realization that "nobody is perfect," that drives individuals to Jesus, the Savior. We will never be converted unless we are convinced that we as individuals are wretched, miserable sinners. And whether or not God uses a tangible crisis to get us to this point, this is the real crisis to which we must come. A crisis of conviction! Have you come to it yourself? Have you realized that, apart from Christ, you are stuck like a stone in the mud?

The encounter

Jacob was convicted of his sin (32:10). But conviction alone could not solve his problems. He still needed God to intervene. And that is exactly what God did (32:24–32)! As night fell, Jacob sent his family away (32:22–23), probably so that, if Esau found him overnight, his family wouldn't have to perish with him. But, in his solitude, it was not Esau who hunted him down, but God! "A man wrestled with him until daybreak" (32:24). Who was that man? Well, in verse 30, Jacob tells us: "I have seen God face to face." Jacob was wrestling with God himself!

And notice how Jacob "wrestled"—intensely. He and the man wrestled "until daybreak" (32:24). What does that mean? Was Jacob wrestling *against* the LORD? No. Jacob was trying to wrestle forgiveness and help *from* the LORD. He was doing, physically, what all of us do, spiritually, when we earnestly pray. He was pleading with God for mercy. He was begging God for it. He was trying to wrestle it out of him: "I will not let you go unless you bless me" (32:26)!

But why did God make Jacob wrestle all night? God could have ended the encounter any time he wanted. All he had to do was "touch" his hip and Jacob was crippled for the rest of his life. So the length of the bout wasn't because it was an even match. Why, then, did Jesus allow Jacob to grapple so long? To see how badly he really wanted the blessing of forgiveness and hope! And, in that sense, Jacob prevailed (32:28). Here is a reminder that undergoing the great change—becoming a Christian—is not always quick and easy. It is not just a matter of repeating a prayer, making a decision, or filling out a card. True conversion often comes only after intense wrestling with God. A new identity in Jesus often comes only after a period of persistently praying like Jacob, "I will not let you go unless you bless me."

> A new identity in Jesus often comes only after a period of persistently praying like Jacob, "I will not let you go unless you bless me."

So let me ask you: Have you wrestled with Jesus and prevailed? I am not saying that everyone's wrestling match will be equally long or intense. We may wrestle ten to twelve hours like Jacob. We may only wrestle ten to twelve minutes. Or we may wrestle ten to twelve weeks or months. But everyone who was ever saved went through a time of wrestling—and came out with a definite peace and assurance in Christ.

The change

The great preacher Martyn Lloyd-Jones was once asked, "What does a person look like who has truly met God?" Alluding to Genesis 32:31, he replied, "He walks with a limp."[1] That is incredibly perceptive, isn't it? After encountering the living Christ, Jacob was forever crippled—both physically and in regard to his ego. He could no longer strut around arrogantly as he had done before. His pride turned to lowliness (33:3). His greed turned to generosity (33:10–11). And his self-reliance had turned into worship (33:20). So we who are professing believers must ask ourselves: Have these things happened to me? Have my habits changed? Have I met the Lord?

Look closely at Genesis 33:20. Here we see Jacob building an altar to the LORD—just as his father and grandfather had done. Why did they build altars? To offer sacrifices. And why did they offer sacrifices? So that the blood of those bulls and goats could remind them of how much they needed a Savior. Jacob had finally realized that he needed someone to die for his sins. And Jacob had also finally decided that the LORD would be *his* God. You may have noticed how, up to this point, Jacob always referred to the LORD as "the God of my father Isaac." He never once called him "the LORD my God." But now, in the naming of this altar, he did so. He called it "El-Elohe-Israel," which means "God, the God of Israel." His name was now Israel. And his God was now the LORD. Jacob finally began to worship the LORD.

Again we must ask ourselves: Have these things happened to me? Is the Lord really *my* God? And have I realized that I desperately needed someone (Jesus!) to die for my sins? If the answers are "yes," then, though we may not have new names, the Lord has granted us, with Jacob, new life!

Like father, like sons

Chapter 34 is a reminder that encounters with God happen individually. Jacob was dramatically changed in chapters 32–33. But his sons remained the same (ch. 34). They were deceitful (34:8–24), murderous (34:25–26), greedy (34:27–29), and arrogant (34:31). And, despite his new heart and his distress over their behavior (34:30), Jacob could not change his boys. God would have to bring them to a crisis of their own, as we will see later. This is another subtle reminder that the new heart—unlike the temporal blessings that passed from Abraham to Isaac, Jacob, and then Jacob's sons—is not passed down genetically. God encounters us individually. And we place our faith in him individually. Like their father, Jacob's sons committed their own sins; and, like Jacob, they would have to make God their own God, independent of their father.

Have you come to that realization—that you were not born Christian? That, as godly as your parents may have been, you must encounter Jesus yourself? That you must trust him yourself? Will you do that today?

Jacob I loved

Before we close out this section, we need to take a brief look at chapters 35–36. Why did God bother to reiterate the promises to Jacob (35:1–15)? To remind us that Jacob, in spite of all the dirty water that had gone under the bridge, *was still* the child of God's promise. God's calling of him was gracious and irreversible. God would do what he said he would do!

But what about the rest of these chapters? Why does God leave us with such a long genealogy of unpronounceable names from 35:23 to 36:43? I think it was to illustrate the same point—that God would do what he said he would do! How does a genealogy illustrate that? Well, when I read the list of names, one thing strikes me: I barely recognize any of the names in the generations of Esau (ch. 36). Their names do not roll off my tongue like the names of Reuben,

Simeon, Levi, Judah, Issachar, Zebulun, Joseph, Benjamin, Dan, Naphtali, Gad, and Asher (ch. 35). I don't know near as much about Esau's sons as I do Jacob's. Why? Because it was Jacob's sons, not Esau's, who were God's chosen ones (Gen. 25:23). Jacob's sons, not Esau's, were the children of promise. And therefore it is Jacob's sons, not Esau's, whose stories are recorded in the Bible and are familiar to me.

Do you see? My familiarity (or lack thereof) with these names is illustrative of the fact that God particularly blessed the family of Jacob and not the family of Esau—just as he said he would do! What a reminder of God's faithfulness! And he is just as faithful to all who are his own. If he is your God, he will do what he said he would do. So I ask you: Is he *your* God? Have you met this God? Have you wrestled with him? And have you prevailed?

For further study ▶

FOR FURTHER STUDY

1. Are there other Bible characters who received new names (or nicknames)? With each one, discuss the reason for the name change. What kind of "new name" would you like God to stamp on your soul?
2. God appears in bodily form in chapter 32. Locate some other Old Testament accounts in which he does so. How is this possible? How do these various occasions prefigure the ministry of Jesus, the Word made flesh?

TO THINK ABOUT AND DISCUSS

1. If you are a believer in Jesus, describe to your small group (or write out for yourself) the way in which you came to faith. How did God bring about a crisis of conviction? Where did you encounter him, and by what means? How has he changed you? Compare notes with others in your group. What are the similarities in all the stories?
2. Talk with a Christian friend or others in your small group about the changes you have seen God make in them since their conversions, or about the changes you see him making even now. Encourage one another with what God has done!

Part 4
Joseph—God meant it for good

(37:1–50:26)

12 Misery and mystery

(37:1–38:30)

In the previous chapters, we have seen, very clearly, that the family of Abraham, Isaac, and Jacob was living under the unparalleled mercy of God.

It was "unparalleled" because no one else on the face of the earth was receiving promises like: "in you all the families of the earth will be blessed" (12:3) or "Two nations are in your womb" (25:23); and it was "mercy" because all that God did and promised was utterly undeserved. Abram twice put his wife in a position of compromise and danger. Isaac did the same, and bred a mutated family through his favoritism. And Jacob was a dishonest, greedy con man. All these facts combine to make the account of this unusual family not a story of godly heritage so much as a story of mercy! Thank God that, in his Son, he is just as merciful to poor, stumbling sinners today!

The misery of sin

But it also needs to be pointed out that, as much as Abraham,

Isaac, and Jacob were under the mercy of God, he still reserved the right to chastise them for their sin! "For those whom the Lord loves He disciplines" (Heb. 12:6). So, very often, the LORD allowed the sins of the Israelite fathers to blow up in their faces. Think of the quarreling that went on between Sarai and Hagar. Was it not the fruit of Abram's sin? The same could be said of the hostility between Jacob and Esau. This kind of enmity would be a natural and expected consequence in any family in which the parents had obvious favorites.

So, as much as God shows mercy to sinners, he also often (because he loves us) makes us absolutely miserable in our sins! Sin—whether we are among God's chosen people or not—is a miserable, spreading, spoiling thing. It is like a cancer that eats, then spreads, then eats some more. God has designed it this way, attaching earthly consequences to our sins, so that the pain might urge us to repent! And if there is anything that is clear in Genesis 37–38, it is the misery of sin. What dissension, pain, lingering guilt, and embarrassment sprang up from the polluted soil of sin in the lives of Jacob and his sons! Notice the misery of sin in the various characters in this portion of God's story:

As much as God shows mercy to sinners, he also often (because he loves us) makes us absolutely miserable in our sins!

Joseph's slavery

Joseph comes across as a spoiled, arrogant, know-it-all

in 37:5–11. He had two dreams, both of which seemed to indicate that one day he would be the patriarch and head of his father's family. One day he would be the one to whom they all would look. Now we must assume that, in some way, the dreams were from God. After all, they were fulfilled in startling detail later in his life.

But the question is: How should Joseph have responded to these dreams? Perhaps he should have taken them as a subtle warning about the place of pride in his own life. It seems that strange dreams are often sent our way to reveal some sinful fixation in our lives. And even beyond that, Joseph certainly should have taken these portents about the future as an opportunity to prepare himself for the leadership role that God was going to give him. These dreams might have signaled him to cultivate concern for this family he would one day lead; to cultivate the humility and wisdom needed in leadership. Instead, he used the dreams simply as wind to further inflate his already puffed-up self-opinion.

Joseph took gifts from God—his dreams—and turned them into tools of self-promotion! And aren't we also prone to take the good gifts of God—our positions, our possessions, our intelligence, our education, our sexuality, our ability to pray—and use them, not for the benefit of others and the glory of God, but only to make ourselves feel better? Think it out. What good gifts has God given *you* which you are tempted to use solely for yourself? As you think it out, notice the obvious: Joseph's

What good gifts has God given *you* which you are tempted to use solely for yourself?

sins came back and bit him! He ended up in a pit, in a slave caravan, and in slavery because he abused the good gifts of God. If he was to be God's leader, he would have to learn humility somehow. So God let him stumble; "whom the Lord loves, He disciplines."

The brothers' guilt

Now yes, in a roundabout way, and through his brothers, Joseph got what God had coming to him. But let's not give the brothers a free pass. Their plan of revenge was even more despicable than was his conceit. In 37:25, we find that, even though they had just dumped their brother in a pit and thought about killing him, they had the callousness of heart to be able to sit down and enjoy a nice meal!

Their blood seems to have run completely cold. God had offered them a way out through the protestations of Reuben (37:21–22). This episode could have ended as nothing more than a prank against their little brother. A mean-spirited prank, but a prank nonetheless. But they did not take God's way of escape. Instead they wallowed in their bitterness, and everything got away from them in the matter of just a few hours! And the same may happen to us who are walking too close to the cliff-edge of some sin.

Notice that the sin of Judah and his brothers haunted them for the rest of their lives. You won't find that here in chapter 37. But read on in the story and you will discover that these brothers never got over the guilt of having sold their youngest brother as a slave—and having deceived their aging father. Oh yes, there is forgiveness with God. If we are in Christ, our sins will not damn us eternally. But they may haunt us as long as we live on this earth.

Yet somewhere, amid all the temptations we face, is a way of escape (1 Cor. 10:13). And what misery we avoid if we take it!

Reuben's regret

You will notice in 37:21–22 that, in the midst of all the madness, the only voice of reason was that of Reuben. It was his voice alone that kept Joseph from being slaughtered on the spot. We should praise him for that. But did you notice, in 37:22, that he was not as bold as he should have been? The rest of the brothers wanted to kill Joseph and throw him into a pit. As the oldest brother, Reuben should have stood up and said, "Listen, I know Joseph has been a pain in the neck, but we're not going to do *anything* to harm him." But he only went half way. To his credit, Reuben said, "Shed no blood." But he still allowed them to throw Joseph into the pit. So yes, Reuben kept Joseph from being killed. But when he had the opportunity to squelch the situation entirely, he buckled.

Reuben had good intentions. But, presumably out of fear of what his brothers might say, he did not fully carry them out. So he stayed in the land of good intentions while his brother was carted off to the land of slavery. And Reuben, like the rest of his brothers, lived with regret the rest of his days. All because he did not stand up for the right when he had the chance! And that regret will follow *us* all of *our* days if we are content to drive in circles through the land of good intentions. Do we intend to share the gospel with that co-worker? Do we intend to stop looking at pornography?

Do we intend to make things right with that estranged family member? Do we intend to begin reading the Bible with our children? Do we intend to someday turn our lives over to Jesus? Now is the time! Good intentions without follow-through lead only to the misery of regret.

All sin, in fact, leads eventually to misery—especially in the lives of God's people. God will not allow us to stay content in sin. And the difficulty of his discipline ought to motivate us to obey!

The mystery of providence

In the events of Genesis 37–38, God seems completely absent from the minds of Jacob and his sons. But that by no means indicates that God was not actively involved in what was happening! Let me ask you: Who was the "man" who directed young Joseph when he was looking for his brothers (37:15–17)? Maybe it was the same "man" who wrestled with Joseph's father back in chapter 32—God himself! Or maybe it was *just* a man. But in either case, it was no accident in Joseph's life that "A man found him" and helped him find his brothers! Just as it was no accident in 37:25 that, at just the right time, a caravan of traders came along to bring Joseph down to Egypt!

That is right! *At just the right time*, those traders came along. Why? Because God wanted Joseph in Egypt! Therefore, God superintended everything that happened in his life to make sure he got there! How do we know that? Well (without giving away the whole story), because, in chapter 50, we learn that God's plan all along was that Joseph might come to power in Egypt and thus keep his family alive when famine hit many years later! God wanted to rescue his chosen people from the impending famine—to keep the bloodline of the Messiah alive. Therefore he sovereignly controlled all the events of Genesis 37—the man in verse 15, the caravan in verse 25, and, yes, even Joseph and his brother's sins—in order to get Joseph to Egypt! Jacob's sons were trying to kill their baby brother. But God was turning their actions into a chain of events that would save their own lives! What mercy!

God truly does cause "all things"—including those seemingly random things; including others' sins against us; and even including our own sins—"to work together for good" to his people (Rom. 8:28)!

Jacob's sons were trying to kill their baby brother. But God was turning their actions into a chain of events that would save their own lives! What mercy!

If we really believe that, then we won't feel the need to throw others into the pit when they hurt us—and we will also have hope in the midst of guilt and regret over our own personal sins. Maybe we weren't the faithful parents we should have been. Maybe we wasted our youth in riotous living. Maybe we didn't speak up for Jesus when we should have. But if we are God's children, we should know this: God works all things—even our failures—for the good of his people. He will work something beautiful out of the mess that we have made.

Now this does not excuse our disobedience—for surely God would rather accomplish his good purposes through obedience rather than sin. But the sovereignty of God over the sins of Joseph and his brothers does teach us that God is bigger than our sins. He is big enough to forgive our sins through Jesus Christ. He is big enough to help us overcome our sins. And he is even big enough to re-work our sins as part of his larger plan to do us, and the rest of his people, good! We may have meant it for evil, but God will work it for good!

Misery and mystery—a close-up

Finally, think of chapter 38 as a close-up version of the wide-angle shot we saw in chapter 37. There we saw sin's misery on a family-wide scale. Here we see it in the life of one member of that family—Judah. Thinking he was beyond the sight of anyone that mattered (and forgetting that "The eyes of the LORD are in every place," Prov. 15:3), Judah spent the night with a prostitute (38:12–16). Little did he know that it was his own daughter-in-law, pushed out onto the streets by his callousness (38:6–11). And, as had been the case with his family—and as is always the case—sin led to misery. Judah's hard-heartedness led to Tamar's prostitution. Her prostitution seduced him into further degradation. And this eventually led to great embarrassment, shame, and guilt. And the same will be true for us. There are no secret sins. God sees them all. And he will bring them out into the open, if necessary, to coax us to repent; "be sure your sin will find you out" (Num. 32:23).

But again, in the midst of the misery, notice the mercy and mystery of God's providence. Out of Judah's incestuous relationship with Tamar were born two sons—Perez and Zerah (38:27–30). Does the name Perez sound familiar? If it doesn't, it should. Both Luke 3:33 and Matthew 1:3 inform us that Perez—the child of incest; the kind of baby who should never have been born—was an ancestor of Jesus, the Messiah!

The Messiah was to be "the Lion … from the tribe of Judah" (Rev. 5:5). It was God's plan that he would come through the family line of this wicked character we've been reading about in Genesis 38. But in 38:7, Judah's oldest son died without a child. In 38:10, his next son died without a child. And in 38:11, Judah kicked his daughter-in-law out of the family. Things weren't looking good for God's messianic plan. Yet in the rest of the chapter, we see the sovereignty of God ensuring that the bloodline of the Messiah would remain intact—even if he had to use the ugliness of Judah and Tamar's sin to make it happen!

Do you see? God is in control; and Jesus is the goal of all human history! God was determined that his Son should be glorified as king! And God was determined that we should have a Savior. Nothing and no one was going to thwart his plan! Not Judah's sin; not anyone's sin against us; not even our own sin. God *will* work all things for the good of his people and the glory of his Son!

FOR FURTHER STUDY

1. Study the Bible's teaching on dreams. How did God use them in biblical times? What are we to make of them today? Are any precautions given regarding dreams? What are they?
2. In Genesis 38:8, Onan is urged to perform his "duty" to his widowed sister-in-law (i.e. to have children with her). What was the biblical principle behind this (see Deut. 25:5–6)? Why do you think God was so angry with Onan's response?

TO THINK ABOUT AND DISCUSS

1. Can you remember a time, as a believer, when God made you miserable in your sin? What was the good outcome of such discipline?
2. Think about a recent temptation you have faced. Did you discern (or can you now see) how God was providing a way of escape (1 Cor. 10:13)? What was it? Did you take it?
3. Share some ways in which you have clearly seen God take a sinful situation and (though not excusing the sin), work it for good. Can you think of some other biblical examples of such mercy?

13 Faithfulness and favor

(39:1–41:57)

"I told God that if I just had five thousand dollars, all my problems would go away. And when I started praying with this prayer cloth ..." That was the message I received in the mail. And it got me thinking. So many religious teachers and followers these days are talking about "the blessing."

Explaining how we may claim this blessing has, in fact, become a multi-million-dollar television and book industry. But one wonders what might be the outcome if the prosperity teachers began to tell folk that "the blessing" of God might not land us five thousand dollars but on a cross, in slavery, or in a prison.

As we pick up again with the life of Joseph in Genesis 39 we will discover that, in spite of his previous arrogance, Joseph was a man clearly under the blessing of God! And yet "the blessing" was not always exactly what we might think. So he is an interesting study if we really want to know what the

Bible says about "the blessing," about the favor of God. Let's follow him along and see what we discover.

The favor of God

There is no question that one of the main emphases of the account of Joseph is the favor of God in his life. In fact, the news that God was with Joseph is repeated eight times in chapter 39 alone:

- "the LORD was with Joseph, so he became a successful man" (39:2)
- "the LORD was with him" (39:3)
- "the LORD caused all that he did to prosper in his hand" (39:3)
- "the LORD blessed the Egyptian's house on account of Joseph" (39:5)
- "the LORD's blessing was upon all that he owned" (39:5)
- "the LORD was with Joseph and extended kindness to him" (39:21)
- "the LORD was with him" (39:23)
- "whatever he did, the LORD made to prosper" (39:23).

The message is clear, isn't it? Even though Joseph was away from his homeland; even though he had been betrayed by his brothers; even though he was no longer a free man; and even though he ended up in prison: still the LORD was with him. To be sure, God eventually brought Joseph full circle and granted blessings that were more obviously blessings (see chapters 40–41). But often God's saints do not experience this turnabout in their situations until the world to come, as Hebrews 11, for instance, makes clear. So let us put away once and for all the idea that God's blessing necessarily equates to health, wealth, and prosperity. That is not the consistent teaching of the Bible. In fact, the Bible and experience often teach exactly the opposite.

On the other hand, let us not deny the fact that, in Genesis 39–41, the blessing of God *was*, in some ways, related to success and prosperity. In Potiphar's house, in the prison, and in Pharaoh's court, God made Joseph successful. God made him, if you will, a good businessman—a wise manager. And we do not discount the fact that the blessing of God may rest on some of us in similar ways. In fact, many of God's people are successful at what they do. God has given them financial security, influence on people, and respect from their peers. But the question is: "Why?"

Well, notice that all of Joseph's prosperity actually funneled into the hands of other people. The fact that Joseph "became a successful man" did not make him personally wealthy. What actually happened was that God's blessing in the life of Joseph made Potiphar personally wealthy (39:5), rescued Pharaoh's kingdom (ch. 41), and preserved Joseph's family through famine (ch. 42 and following). That's interesting, isn't it? Even when God was blessing Joseph with great success and power, it was not about Joseph's health, wealth, and prosperity. God blessed Joseph so that Joseph could be a constant blessing to others! Furthermore, God prospered Joseph so that he might have a testimony for the LORD in high places. Because of his success as a manager, Joseph was able to influence

God blessed Joseph so that Joseph could be a constant blessing to others!

Potiphar, the chief jailer, and eventually Pharaoh himself for the LORD!

Most of us are not exactly like Joseph—serving high up in the government, or impacting a nation's finances. But in our spheres of influence, are we using the manifest blessings of God (be they influence, position, popularity, or money) to bless others and speak for God? Think of it like this: What would you do if God really did send you a five-thousand-dollar check in the mail? Would you immediately get about alleviating the misery of others, blessing the missionaries, or helping your church complete its building campaign? Or would you simply burn it up, making all *your* problems go away?

The faithfulness of Joseph

It goes without saying—and it follows all we have just said—that those who are under the *favor* of God are expected to demonstrate *faithfulness* to God. And Joseph certainly did! Take a closer look:

Joseph's integrity

Scanning over 39:1–6, we observe the great faithfulness with which Joseph served in Potiphar's house. He was worthy of notice (39:3) and eventually of promotion (39:4). In fact, his integrity under Potiphar is summed up in verse 6: "[Potiphar] did not concern himself with anything except the food he ate." Literally, the Hebrew says, Potiphar "did not *know* what was in his house." He did not need to. After all, Joseph would take care of things!

What a challenge Joseph is to us! Are we known as the

most trustworthy employees in our workplaces? Would our bosses entrust us with their checkbooks? Can we be trusted to be on time, and to obey orders? These are the kinds of believers—the Josephs of the world—whom God uses to adorn the gospel and attract unbelievers to himself.

Joseph's chastity

Potiphar so trusted Joseph that he left him alone at home with his wife. Again I ask: Is this true of us? Can we be trusted alone with another man's wife or husband, or daughter or son? Can we be trusted alone on the internet? Joseph could be trusted! But notice that, even though he was trustworthy, he went an extra mile in fleeing temptation. Day after day, Potiphar's wife would put on her perfume, bat her eyelashes, and urge Joseph to give in to her seduction. But day after day, Joseph would refuse "to listen to her to lie beside her or [even to] *be with her*" (39:10). There is the practical key to Joseph's sexual purity—he refused even to "be with her"! He took great pains to make sure they were never alone together. That is why verse 11 makes a point of noting that, on one particular day, it did not work out that way.

Isn't this a stark contrast from what we saw in Joseph's brother Judah in chapter 38? Judah walked right up to the seductress; Joseph avoided her altogether. What about you? Do you take great pains not to be alone with a member of the opposite sex? This is the only sure way to avoid temptation—and false accusation.

Joseph's industry

Notice how Joseph, when it came to the gift of interpreting

dreams, did not bury his talent in the ground! This may not seem all that extraordinary once he was out of prison and standing before Pharaoh. After all, if you or I had an opportunity to impress the CEO of our companies or stand before Congress, we probably would not slouch around either! But remember that this audience with Pharaoh (ch. 41) was precipitated by his faithful use of his gift in a very different setting—the jailhouse (ch. 40)! There Joseph was—in prison and falsely accused. But in the form of the cupbearer and baker, along came the opportunity to put his spiritual gift to work. What would you have done? I'll tell you what might have gone through my mind: "I'm not going to go out of my way trying to help these two. Nobody appreciates me around here, anyway. Potiphar wouldn't listen to me. His wife betrayed me. These Egyptians are all the same. Why should I go out of my way to help these two criminals?"

Joseph's audience with Pharaoh was precipitated by his faithful use of his gift in a very different setting—the jailhouse!

Perhaps this is precisely where some of us are in our churches, small groups, or careers—jaded, disillusioned, or discouraged. So we have decided that we will no longer serve on the committee, no longer speak up on that issue, no longer be a member of the team, no longer teach the class. If that describes you, take a long look at Joseph. Lying in that jailhouse he had every excuse in the world just to roll over and play spiritually dead. He had every excuse to bury his talent in the ground. But he didn't. Instead, he stayed committed to the LORD; he used his spiritual gift; and eventually God used that gift to get him into the throne room of Pharaoh! And God would do similar things with us if we would only serve him without losing heart!

Joseph's wisdom

What an amazing plan Joseph came up with in 41:33–36! An engineer could hardly have done better. But where did Joseph get his agricultural wisdom? Was he trained by his father? Did he pick it up in the midst of all his labors as a slave? We are not sure. It is possible that it was given, miraculously, by God. But more often than not, the wisdom that comes from above comes to us as a result of our applying ourselves hard to study. And, somewhere along the line, it would seem, Joseph had done this. He had applied himself to the agricultural branch of learning—and God blessed that knowledge to the rescue of many souls (41:54).

Now this is certainly a mandate for Christians to imitate Joseph, excelling in all kinds of wisdom—agriculture, medicine, science, history, etc.—and using that wisdom to bless mankind and to honor the Lord. In a very real sense, Joseph's life teaches us to use our careers, skills, and gifts to serve the Lord by serving others. But it should be pointed out that there is another kind of wisdom which may be used to rescue the perishing, eternally. Paul calls it "the wisdom that leads to salvation through faith which is in Christ Jesus," and says it is a wisdom found only in "the sacred writings" (2 Tim. 3:15). Thus, one application for us would be to apply ourselves to learning the gospel—to being able (and, of course, willing) to share the good news of Jesus clearly, fully, and accurately at a moment's notice. Can you do that? If not, you have homework! Who knows but that God may put you in a position, even this week, to rescue someone from eternal death! Will you have acquired the wisdom to do so?

Which came first?

The two main portraits in Genesis 39–41 show the favor of God and the faithfulness of Joseph. But which came first? Was it that the faithfulness of Joseph resulted in the favor of God? Or was it that the favor of God gave rise to the faithfulness of Joseph? Or was it both?

Was it God's favor that led to the faithfulness of Joseph? Very clearly, yes! For when we saw Joseph in chapter 37, he was an arrogant, mouthy teenage boy. And the very next thing we read about him (39:2) is that "The LORD was with Joseph." God's initial favor towards Joseph was not a result of goodness in Joseph (for he had shown none), but of the grace of God! And it was only after we read that "The LORD was with Joseph" that we begin to see Joseph act as though *he* was with the LORD. Joseph's faithfulness was a flower that bloomed only after much plowing, planting, and watering on the LORD's part. And this is the way it works with all of us. None of us is faithful to God on our own. It is only once we have been shown God's favor—once we have been united to Jesus—that we are able to respond with faithfulness. "For we are *His workmanship*, created in Christ Jesus for good works, *which God prepared beforehand* so that we would walk in them" (Eph. 2:10). God's favor leads to our faithfulness. And, whenever we find ourselves doing right, we would all do well to take up the mantra of Joseph: "It is not in me; God ..." (41:16).

But it would, in some ways, be right to say that our faithfulness is rewarded with God's favor. Jesus himself illustrated this in the parable of the talents (Matt. 25). Those who are faithful in little things are blessed with greater responsibilities. This principle is illustrated over and again in the life of Joseph, isn't it? He was faithful as a mere slave, so God made him the personal assistant of Potiphar (39:4). He was faithful in the prison, so God made him master of the prison (39:22). He was faithful as the master of the prison (ch. 40), so God made him second in command to Pharaoh (ch. 41). Do you see the principle? "Those who honor Me I will honor," declares the LORD (1 Sam. 2:30). Our faithfulness *is* rewarded with God's favor.

So which comes first: our faithfulness or God's favor? If we look carefully at this story, and at the Bible in general, we discover that the answer is "both." In both cases, however, the final credit belongs to God. After all, "we are *His* workmanship."

FOR FURTHER STUDY

1. Jesus speaks about God's favor, or blessing, in Matthew 5:1–12. How do these qualities compare with the more modern, popular ideas about God's "blessing"? Which of these qualities do we see reflected in the life of Joseph? How? Which would you like to see reflected in your own life?
2. Ancient rabbis expected the Messiah to be the "son of Joseph," that is, they believed that Joseph, in all his trials and triumphs, was a prefiguring of what the Messiah would be like. Look back over the life of Joseph (and do some thinking ahead, too). In which ways does Joseph prefigure the trials, triumphs, and characteristics of Jesus? In which ways is Jesus greater than Joseph?

TO THINK ABOUT AND DISCUSS

1. Where and when have you encountered the so-called "prosperity gospel"? Aside from its unbiblical view of suffering, what other problems does it present: in evangelism? in dealing with the poor? theologically?
2. In what specific ways has God outwardly blessed you? How have you seen God use your position, talent, finances, etc., to promote his glory? How might you leverage these gifts to go even further for his cause?
3. We observed Joseph's integrity, chastity, industry, and wisdom. Which quality speaks loudest to you as a matter for personal prayer and sanctification? Why?

14 Change is good

(42:1–45:28)

2 Corinthians 5:17 says that "if anyone is in Christ, he is a new creature; the old things passed away; behold, new things have come." Isn't that a wonderful promise? As believers in Jesus, we no longer have to keep on living as we once did. A great change has come over us.

This newness does not necessarily become observable overnight. Often God works our sanctification over extended periods and through prolonged circumstances. But the change eventually becomes obvious. It is wonderful when we observe how God is changing new (or seasoned) Christians in our churches. And it is wonderful to look back on our own lives, to remember what we once were, and to see that God has brought about real change! Such observation is a great aid to our assurance. The "new creature" that we have become (and are becoming) is evidence that we are, indeed, "in Christ"!

And what we observe happening in Genesis 42–45 demonstrates that new creatures are by no means only a New Testament phenomenon. In fact, we might even go so far as to say that these chapters present, in biographical form, what 2 Corinthians 5 teaches in doctrinal form. As the preincarnate Christ worked in the lives of this family, its members became changed! They were becoming God's new creatures! Let's observe that together.

Change is needed

Now, in the previous chapter we observed that a change seemed already to have been afoot in Joseph. It seems that God had used the oil of affliction to soften his heart and change his outlook. But, as we see in chapters 42–45, there was still work to be done. And if that was true of Joseph, it was also true of his father and brothers. Let's look at three family portraits from chapter 42 to demonstrate the need for change in these various men.

Forgotten but not forgiven

Sometimes we salve our consciences by telling ourselves that it is all right to forgive someone but not necessarily to forget what he or she did. This is just an unbiblical way of harboring continued bitterness. (Compare what God teaches us about his own manner of forgiveness—Isa. 43:25; Jer. 31:34—with the command to forgive "as God in Christ also has forgiven you," Eph. 4:32.) But there is an even more serious error. While some of us convince ourselves that we have forgiven without forgetting, others of us make no pretense of forgiveness. We do not want to forgive. We just want to cut the offenders out of our lives and pretend they do not exist anymore. We want to forget so we do not have to forgive!

That was Joseph. Look back at 41:50–51: "Now before the year of famine came, two sons were born to Joseph, whom Asenath, the daughter of Potiphera priest of On, bore to him. Joseph named the firstborn Manasseh, 'For,' he said, 'God has made me forget all my trouble and all my father's household.'" Joseph had forgotten his brothers. And the heavy-handedness with which he treated them in chapter 42 showed that he had forgotten without forgiving. And we are prone to the same, aren't we? Sometimes it is easier to cut off a family member or friend than to forgive him or her. So we forget, but do not forgive. And we need a change.

Sometimes it is easier to cut off a family member or friend than to forgive him or her. So we forget, but do not forgive.

Guilty but not forgiven

There are those who convince themselves they have forgiven but not forgotten. There are others who have forgotten but not forgiven. And then there are those who, like Joseph's brothers, need to experience forgiveness themselves! Notice how burdened with guilt they were: "Truly we are guilty concerning our brother … therefore this distress has come upon us" (42:21); and "Now comes the reckoning for his blood" (42:22). Notice, especially, how they responded to an apparent kindness of God in 42:28: "What is this that God has done to us?" That is what happens when you have a guilty conscience! Even the kindness of God seems to call you to account!

These men were guilty—and they knew it. Yet, unlike those who know they are guilty and have experienced the peace of Jesus, these men did not feel forgiven. Indeed, they could not. They had never dealt with their sin. Even though 42:36 shows that Jacob now had some inkling about what had happened to his son, we are given no indication that Joseph's brothers had yet confessed their sins and sought their father's forgiveness. And their obvious fear of God's judgment in 42:22 and 28 shows that they had never brought their sins before *the Lord* to request and receive *his* forgiveness. So Joseph's brothers teach us a valuable lesson. Just because we feel convicted over our sins, it doesn't necessarily mean that we are forgiven! We may feel as guilty as we like, but, until we bring our sins to God and confess, we cannot be forgiven. That is where Joseph's brothers were stuck in chapter 42. And they needed a change. So, perhaps, do some of us.

Neither forgiven nor forgotten

That is the phrase to describe Jacob's response to his sons' treachery. At least twenty years had passed since Joseph had disappeared, presumed to have been eaten by wild beasts. But Jacob (as 42:36 shows us) had never gotten over it. Now, I suppose that no one ever really fully gets over the loss of a child. And I am not sure that we are supposed to. So it is not Jacob's sadness over Joseph that was sinful. Jacob's sin was in the fact that *he still hadn't forgiven his sons* for whatever role they might have played in Joseph's supposed death. Time should have allowed his wounds to heal and his bitterness to die. Instead, his unforgiveness festered for two decades.

But notice a second way Jacob responded to losing Joseph. He responded to losing one favorite son by crowning another—Benjamin—as his new favorite. His initial (and obvious) favoritism towards Joseph had been patently sinful. But, in losing Joseph, he was given a chance to recognize that and repent. Instead, he salved his wound by picking another favorite—by continuing in the very same sin! That may sound familiar to us. So many times, when God takes away one sinful habit, we simply replace it with another equally sinful habit. And we, like Jacob, need a change!

Change is good

Joseph needed to forgive. His brothers needed to confess and be forgiven. And their father needed to forgive, forget, and lay down his favoritism. And, in chapters 43–45, we find that God, through extraordinary difficulties and surprises, performed the work! And again, this family serves as an example to us. It reminds us, not only that we need changing, but also that God wants to change us—and that God has many ways of getting our attention and melting our hearts. Notice three more family portraits, this time of godly change.

Jacob went from favoritism to faith

When Jacob had lost his favorite son Joseph, he had simply replaced him with another idol, Benjamin. That is why he was so stubborn about sending the boys back to Egypt. He was afraid to lose Benjamin. He was afraid to let go of his idol. But finally, in 43:13, he let him go! And what did God use to change his heart? Famine! Jacob didn't want to let go of Benjamin. So he held on, and held on, and held on—until circumstances forced him to make a radical decision. Either he could hold onto his idol and risk losing his whole family to starvation, or he could let go of Benjamin and trust God to fill the void. And he chose, finally, to let go and trust God (43:13–14)! Finally, it was "God Almighty" and not his youngest son that brought Jacob comfort.

Here is a lesson in the ways of God. Sometimes he brings against us great hardships (like famine) to bring us to repentance. Sometimes he breaks our arms to force us to let go of our idols. That is the way many people are initially brought to Christ—through great physical or emotional suffering! And it is certainly the way in which God often works out change in the lives of his followers—through suffering! But the change God brings about is worth pain! Jacob finished his life a changed man! His bitterness was gone. His family was a family again. But it took famine to get there.

Joseph's brothers went from bitterness to bravery

Joseph's brothers finally learned to love (44:14–34)! Wasn't that their problem all along? They did not love Joseph. And they did not seem to love their father, either. But now look at Judah (44:33)—representing, I think, the sentiments of the other nine—on his knees, begging for their brother's life. They had gone from selling their spoiled brother into slavery to being willing to sell themselves into slavery to save another spoiled brother!

How did God do it? First, through guilt. Everywhere they

turned, they seemed to see Joseph's face—even though they didn't recognize him standing right in front of them. Their sins seemed to be haunting them. I think that is why they said what they did in 44:16: "What can we say to my lord? What can we speak? And how can we justify ourselves? God has found out the iniquity of your servants." They knew they weren't guilty of stealing the cup. What they meant, it seems, was that God was paying them back for their treatment of Joseph so many years before. They deserved the rough treatment they were now getting—not because of the cup, but because of the pit into which they had thrown Joseph. And they weren't going to make that mistake again. Thus, the healthy guilt we see in 44:16 brought them, finally, to repentance!

But God also brought about the brothers' change, I believe, through the change in their father. Notice 43:14 again. For years, Jacob had only cared about Joseph. Then, for years, he had only cared about Benjamin. In fact, as we see in 42:38, Jacob had a tendency to speak as if he only had one son. But in 43:14, he finally speaks of his "children," plural: "if I am bereaved of my *children*, I am bereaved." It seems as if Jacob had finally begun to care for *all* his boys. He had begun to repent of his favoritism—and his sons noticed! Isn't that why they were so protective of their little brother in chapter 44—because of their affection for their father? "For the sake of our father, preserve the boy's life" is Judah's consistent plea.

Jacob's repentance set off a chain reaction that, by the end of the story, had resulted in changed lives for his eleven older sons. So let me apply this just by pointing out that this kind of domino effect can be used by God today. Very often, God will use a radical change in one person's life to touch the lives of many other people and bring them to similar change. And he might just do it in our families and workplaces if we would forgive, repent, or make things right again!

Very often, God will use a radical change in one person's life to touch the lives of many other people and bring them to similar change.

Joseph went from frustration to forgiveness

Finally, after all his angry posturing towards his brothers, Joseph broke down (45:1–5). He revealed his identity to them. And he urged them not to be afraid, for they were forgiven, and should forgive themselves (44:5). What was the catalyst? The example of Judah's love (44:18–34). Just as his brothers had seen the change in their father and been changed themselves, so Joseph saw the change in Judah and his hard heart was broken wide open. Judah (and the other brothers), who had so mistreated him, was now willing to lay down his life for his youngest brother. That kind of love catches people's attention. And that is a good word for those of us who have family members and friends who are hard-hearted towards us or towards the gospel. Keep loving. Keep sharing the good news … and watch God eventually break through!

Changing places

Do you remember Judah at the end of chapter 44, pleading for his youngest brother's life? "Let me change places with him. Let me take the punishment that hangs over his head! Let me be taken so that he might go free." Isn't this a beautiful picture of what Jesus has done for us? Isn't this amazing love—that a man would trade his life in exchange for his brother's? That is what Judah wanted to do for Benjamin. And that is what Christ did on the cross. This is why we may become God's children and enter into this process whereby God works all sorts of circumstances to change us into his image.

We began this chapter with 2 Corinthians 5, and I'd like to invite you to turn there again to firm up this final point. Immediately after describing the new creature in 5:17, Paul says, "Now all these things are from God, who reconciled us to Himself through Christ" (5:18). In other words, being a "new creature" is "from God." You don't become a new creature by trying to do better, by making resolves, or by pulling up your spiritual bootstraps. *God* makes you a new creature! He works out the change, as we have seen, through various circumstances. But he always begins it in the same way: by reconciling us "to Himself through Christ."

> You don't become a new creature by trying to do better, by making resolves, or by pulling up your spiritual bootstraps. *God* makes you a new creature!

And how, exactly, does God reconcile us to himself "through Christ"? Read 2 Corinthians 5:21: "He made Him who knew no sin to be sin on our behalf, so that we might become the righteousness of God in Him." How do you become reconciled to God and thus begin this process of becoming a new, changed creature? By having changed places with Jesus (as Benjamin might have done with Judah)! And that is the biggest change of all! He has taken on the sin that we committed, gone to the cross that was made for us, and died the death that we deserved! And, in exchange, we are treated as though we had earned the righteousness that he earned; we are given the new life that he possessed; and we inherit the heaven that he alone deserves! We can be changed into new creatures because Jesus has changed places with us!

For further study ▶

FOR FURTHER STUDY

1. Re-read 2 Corinthians 5:17–21. I have referred to the phrase "new creature" mainly to describe the ongoing process of sanctification that God works in the life of the believer. Do these verses, however, also have something to say regarding our justification (i.e. the immediate benefits of trusting Christ)? What is the difference between justification and sanctification?2. I mentioned Ephesians 4:32, in which we are taught to forgive because God has forgiven us. What else does the New Testament teach about our forgiving of one another? Do a study on this concept. What surprises you? Is there anyone you need to forgive before it is too late?

TO THINK ABOUT AND DISCUSS

1. How can we go about forgiving *and* forgetting the offense of another person? What does it mean to forget someone's sins? What does God mean when he speaks this way about himself (Isa. 43:25; Jer. 31:34)?

2. Skim back over chapters 42–45. What were some of the positive effects of the changes God brought about in the lives of Jacob and his sons: within their own family? on the onlooking world (think particularly about 45:2)? How have you seen God use changes in yourself to positively affect others? How have the changes he has effected in others been a blessing to you?

15 Finishing well

(46:1–50:26)

Eric Liddell, Olympic Champion-turned-missionary to China, was made world famous by the movie *Chariots of Fire*. In a particularly poignant scene in the film, Liddell falls down just a few strides into a 440-yard race. The crowd groans. His hopes for a medal seem dashed. But to their amazement, Liddell rises to his feet, leans his head back in characteristic fashion, strides even harder, and catches his opponents from twenty yards back to win the race.

This became Liddell's signature—not the way he began his races, but the way he finished: head tilted back, mouth wide open, body in full stretch, and feet moving faster than those of any other man in the world! He is a classic portrait of the adage "It's not how you begin the race but how you finish that is important."

How true that is in the Christian life! None of us begins

very well. We begin as sinners, desperately in need of God's grace. But even when we come to Christ, receive forgiveness, and begin running the race set before us (Heb. 12:1), we find that our gait is often characterized by fits and starts. We do not always proceed as smoothly or as rapidly as we would like. But we realize that, while the way in which we run the race *is* important, what is most important is how we finish. Will we give up? Will we simply coast to the finish line? Or will we run into the arms of Jesus with our heads tilted back and our souls in full stretch?

While the way in which we run the race *is* important, what is most important is how we finish.

Jacob was a man who ran not unlike many of us. Way back in Genesis 32, Jacob met God and began running well. His eyes were focused on the LORD. His previously crooked pathway had been straightened out. But over time—probably much more gradually than we realize from reading his life in print—Jacob and his sons began to lose focus. Family squabbles, the loss of a son, and year after year of guilt and unforgiveness had knocked them so far off track that we would never have discerned that they were the people of God if we had picked up the story, say, in chapter 37.

Jacob's family had run completely off course. But God, in his mercy, used the goads of reconciliation and repentance to prod them back onto their feet, to get them running, and to help them finish well. So much so that, in chapters 46–50, it almost seems as if we are reading about an entirely different family! Jacob's sons, who, just a few chapters ago, had been fearful and indecisive (42:1), were now leading their families with strength and surety (46:5). Jacob, who (as we observed him in the last few chapters) had become a blubbering old man, was now able to stand with dignity and grace before the most powerful man in the world (47:9) and pray for him! This family, which seemed to have almost forgotten its role as the chosen people of God, was now recognizing and embracing that role once again. And Jacob, who had been worshiping at the altar of his favorite son for over two decades, was now back worshiping at the altar of the LORD (46:1)!

The entire family seems to have gained new strength for the race. And particularly, in these final chapters we get to see two members cross the tape, heads back and souls fully stretched out in faith in the LORD.

Jacob's last words

Chapters 47–49 record the last few hours of Jacob's life. How well he finished! In fact, his dying words are some of the most memorable in the Bible. Notice, for instance, that Jacob was adamant about being buried back home in the land of Canaan (47:29–31). Why was this so important to him? Well, because Canaan was the land of promise. Canaan was God's land, and Jacob and his family were God's people. So Jacob wanted even his burial to be a testament to the fact that the LORD was his God! That is instructive, isn't it? Jacob was so concerned to leave behind a testimony for the LORD that even the arrangements for his funeral were important to him! What a spur he could be for many of us! Westerners are often very concerned to have all the practical details of a funeral worked out—the casket, the burial plot, the funeral home—but spend very little time thinking about how this funeral service can speak for the Lord. Christians (and their believing families) ought to be different. We ought to labor to make funerals an opportunity for the preaching of the gospel and worshiping of the Lord. That was what Jacob was thinking on his deathbed: "How can my death point my family to God?"

But Jacob went further. He had more to say than simply to give his funeral requests. Notice 48:3. When he had gotten to the very end, he called his son Joseph to his bedside, and the first words out of his mouth were "God Almighty." He then proceeded to recount the blessings and promises of God. And again, this is instructive, because it is (sadly!) so different from how most people operate. What do most people talk about when they are lying sick in the hospital bed? They talk about their sickness—the treatments, the medicines, the pain, the doctors, and so on! You go to visit them and it is as though there is nothing happening in the universe besides their sickness. You read the Bible to them, and they go right back to talking about their sickness. You ask about their family, and they use it as an opportunity to get back to bemoaning their sickness. But, as Christians, we have something altogether more hopeful and more important to talk about! Namely, "God Almighty," and what great things he has done for us!

So both in his burial request and in his last conversation with Joseph, Jacob was using the last moments of his life to remind his family of their commitments to God! That is why he was buried where he was buried, and why he spoke the way he spoke—so that he might give one last testimony to encourage his sons to follow the LORD with all their hearts! Jacob's desire to give a final testimony is also the reason why he called in Joseph's sons (48:8–22)—and eventually brought together all of his children (ch. 49)—to pronounce God's blessings upon them. What a beautiful way for Jacob to die!

So let me just ask again: Are you going to die that way? Are you going to finish well? Since life is so uncertain and our years are so "few" (47:9), there is no better time to get into our closing sprints than now! If we want to finish well, we must run well now! We must speak much of Jesus now! We must pass the gospel along to our families now! We must gather them together for prayer now! We must serve the Lord now!

You see, the key to Jacob's happy ending was not mainly that he was happy. That was most obvious. He was thrilled to have his whole family together again. But that is not what was most important. What was important was that he finished his life in an all-out sprint, serving the LORD. Murmuring had been replaced with praise. Accusations had been replaced with blessings. Passivity and reclusiveness had been replaced with action. And fear had been replaced with faith (46:4)! Jacob had finished well.

Joseph's tombstone

The book of Genesis closes with the death of Joseph, the hero of its final chapters. Like his father, Joseph finished well. He reminded his brothers of God's providence (50:20) and his own forgiveness (50:21). And, like his father, he asked to be buried, not in Egypt, but in God's country—Canaan. Generations later his request was fulfilled as Moses carried his bones up from Egypt in the Exodus (Exod. 13:19) and

Joshua, eventually, buried them in Jacob's field in Shechem (Josh. 24:32). We aren't given any more details than that about Joseph's burial. Was there a ceremony? Did someone give a eulogy of this great father in the faith? If so, what did that person say? Was there a marker at the grave? All these questions remain unanswered.

But let's suppose for a moment that there was a grave marker set up in the field in Shechem. What might have been written under the name "Joseph" on such a stone? Well, there is usually only space for one brief phrase, or maybe a sentence at most. So we usually see phrases like "BELOVED HUSBAND," "FAITHFUL MOTHER," and so on. Whatever words we might place on someone's tombstone, they must be brief, and they ought, in a very pointed way, to tell us something important about the person buried below.

So, given that set of guidelines, what might we have engraved on Joseph's gravestone? What was the main theme of his life? And how would we state it? What would we put on Joseph's tombstone? Perhaps this simple phrase: "GOD MEANT IT FOR GOOD." How appropriate to take Joseph's exact words from 50:20 and have them written on his grave marker! Because this is the main lesson of Joseph's life: "God meant it for good." So much heartache, frustration, and wrong dots the timeline of Joseph's 110 years. But in all of this, "God meant it for good."

In 50:20, Joseph was specifically reminding his brothers that, though they "meant evil against" him when they sold him into slavery, "God meant it for good in order to … preserve many people alive" through the seven years of famine. Think through the chain of events that Joseph was encapsulating in that verse, and think how they worked out for good:

- Had Joseph not been sold into slavery, he would never have ended up in Egypt.
- Had Joseph not ended up in Egypt, he would never have gained distinction in Potiphar's house.
- Had he not gained distinction in Potiphar's house, he would never have been falsely accused by Potiphar's wife.
- Had he not been falsely accused by Potiphar's wife, he would never have ended up in jail.

So far, things do not seem to be working out for good! But think on …

- Had Joseph not ended up in jail, he would never have interpreted the cupbearer's dream.
- Had he not interpreted the cupbearer's dream, he would never have been called upon to interpret Pharaoh's dream.
- Had he not interpreted Pharaoh's dream, Egypt would never have been prepared for the coming famine.
- Had Egypt not been prepared for the coming famine, many in Egypt would have died—and so would Joseph and his brothers!
- And had Joseph and his brothers died, there would have been no Israel and, therefore, no Messiah!

Joseph's whole life is one long trail of evidence that demonstrates how God uses the worst of circumstances to turn our lives into something useful and profitable! And the profit of Joseph's suffering continues down to this very day! As believers in Jesus, we benefit from the fact that Joseph's

Joseph's whole life is one long trail of evidence that demonstrates how God uses the worst of circumstances to turn our lives into something useful and profitable!

suffering kept the family tree of the Savior alive! "God causes all things to work together for good to those who love God, to those who are called according to His purpose" (Rom. 8:28)!

The practical applications of this discovery are many. We learn that, even when others are harming us, they are, unwittingly, doing us good—and therefore we can forgive, as Joseph did! We learn that God is in control, and can be trusted even in the darkest hours. And we learn not to judge our circumstances too quickly! If Joseph had measured God's love simply by what he could see in the here and now, he would have lost his faith long before he ever got to chapter 50!

How much more spiritually healthy we would be if we could get Joseph's epitaph, "GOD MEANT IT FOR GOOD," engraved onto our hearts! So much of the Christian life is wrapped up in believing this truth! The ability to forgive is attached to our acceptance of Genesis 50:20. The ability to cope with hardship is tied up in believing Genesis 50:20. The question of why God permits evil is directly related to Genesis 50:20. This is an inestimably important verse and lesson.

Even understanding the gospel itself is difficult if we do not understand and believe the message of Genesis 50:20. For skeptics sometimes ask, "If God is really all-powerful, and if God is really loving, and if Jesus was really God's Son … how could an all-powerful God allow his own Son to be murdered so gruesomely?" The answer is the same as in Genesis 50:20, isn't it? "[They] meant evil against [him], but God meant it for good in order to ... preserve many people alive." The story of Joseph is so much like the story of Jesus! In both cases, God allowed one man to go through tremendous suffering in order, in the end, to bring about rescue for all God's people! This is simply the way God works. If you are God's child, and if you suffer, God means it for good! And knowing such should keep us calm when we are the ones experiencing the suffering.

So when you struggle and when you suffer, remember Joseph. Remember that his brothers meant evil against him, "but God meant it for good." And more than that, remember Jesus—whose suffering was more excruciating than anything you or I will endure, yet who brought about the world's greatest good! Remember the death of Jesus, and all the good it brought about, and you will be able to sing with faith,

Judge not the Lord by feeble sense,
But trust him for his grace;
Behind a frowning providence
He hides a smiling face![1]

For further study ▶

FOR FURTHER STUDY

1. Look back over chapter 49. Is there any significance to the varied blessings pronounced by Jacob over his different sons? How do we see these blessings played out in Scripture? In particular, what significance is attached to the blessing of Judah (49:8–12)?
2. Joseph's life can be summarized by the phrase "you meant evil against me, but God meant it for good." Can you think of some other biblical characters who could have said the same thing? What does this teach us about: God's sovereignty? human sin?

TO THINK ABOUT AND DISCUSS

1. Have there been instances in your life when someone clearly meant evil against you? Have you seen, in retrospect, God working those events for your good and his glory? In what ways? Have you been able to forgive the offender as Joseph forgave his brothers? Is there, perhaps, an appropriate way for you to let that person know he or she is forgiven?
2. Have you been to a funeral that was particularly honoring to the Lord—that of someone who finished as well as Jacob? What elements were present? What typical elements were, perhaps, left out? How might you, like Jacob, prepare for your own death and burial to preach the goodness of the Lord?

Endnotes

Chapter 1

1 For more scientific corroboration of the biblical creation accounts, use the search function at answersingenesis.org.

2 Matthew Henry, *Commentary on the Whole Bible* (McClean, VA: MacDonald Publishers, n.d.), p. 20.

3 Emphasis in all Scripture quotations is mine.

Chapter 2

1 Particularly helpful to me in writing this last section was Peter Williams, *From Eden to Egypt* (Epsom: Day One, 2001), pp. 353–356.

Chapter 3

1 A few reasons why I hold to the view that the "sons of God" were human beings, not fallen angels: 1. Isa. 43:6, Hosea 1:10, and Rom. 8:14 all use the phrase "sons of God" to refer to faithful human beings. Only the book of Job clearly uses the phrase to refer to angels. 2. The "sons of God" were married (v. 2), while Jesus says that angels cannot be married (Matt. 22:30). 3. It is highly unlikely that angels, being bodiless, could have intercourse with and impregnate women who have bodies. 4. The argument of Romans 5 is clearly that Adam is the father of all the living. Introducing a half-human, half-angelic race would call Paul's argument into serious question.

Chapter 4

1 Most of the historo-geographical information in this section (particularly on the line of Japheth) comes from Kenneth Matthews, *The New American Commentary: Genesis 1:1–1:26* (Nashville: Broadman and Holman, 1996), pp. 439–465.

Chapter 5

1 The promise of a "great nation" is reiterated and given a geographic emphasis in 17:1–8.

Chapter 6

1 Williams, *From Eden to Egypt*, p. 85.

2 See NASB footnotes for English translations of the names Abram, Abraham, and Sarah.

Chapter 7

1 Ibid., pp. 97–103. Williams does a wonderful job of pointing out Lot's spiritual and moral confusion.

Chapter 8

1 Sharon James, *My Heart in His Hands: Ann Judson of Burma* (Webster, NY: Evangelical Press, 1998), pp. 343–345.

Chapter 11

1 This quote comes from an interview with Lloyd-Jones's daughter, Lady Elizabeth Catherwood. The interview was recorded by 9 Marks Ministries and can be found within the Audio section at 9marks.org.

Chapter 15

1 William Cowper, "God Moves in a Mysterious Way."

Opening up series

Title	Author	ISBN
Opening up 1 Corinthians	Derek Prime	978–1–84625–004–0
Opening up 1 Thessalonians	Tim Shenton	978–1–84625–031–6
Opening up 1 Timothy	Simon J Robinson	978–1–903087–69–5
Opening up 2 & 3 John	Terence Peter Crosby	978–1–84625–023–1
Opening up 2 Peter	Clive Anderson	978–1–84625–077–4
Opening up 2 Thessalonians	Ian McNaughton	978–1–84625–117–7
Opening up 2 Timothy	Peter Williams	978–1–84625–065–1
Opening up Amos	Michael Bentley	978–1–84625–041–5
Opening up Colossians & Philemon	Ian McNaughton	978–1–84625–016–3
Opening up Ecclesiastes	Jim Winter	978–1–903087–86–2
Opening up Exodus	Iain D Campbell	978–1–84625–029–3
Opening up Ezekiel's visions	Peter Jeffery	978–1–903087–66–4
Opening up Ezra	Peter Williams	978–1–84625–022–4
Opening up Haggai	Peter Williams	978–1–84625–144–3
Opening up Hebrews	Philip Hacking	978–1–84625–042–2
Opening up James	Roger Ellsworth	978–1–84625–165–8
Opening up Jonah	Paul Mackrell	978–1–84625–080–4
Opening up Joshua	Roger Ellsworth	978–1–84625–118–4
Opening up Judges	Simon J Robinson	978–1–84625–043–9
Opening up Luke's Gospel	Gavin Childress	978–1–84625–030–9
Opening up Malachi	Roger Ellsworth	978–1–84625–033–0

Opening up Matthew	Iain D Campbell	978–1–84625–116–0
Opening up Nahum	Clive Anderson	978–1–903087–74–9
Opening up Philippians	Roger Ellsworth	978–1–903087–64–0
Opening up Proverbs	Jim Newheiser	978–1–84625–110–8
Opening up Psalms	Roger Ellsworth	978–1–84625–005–7
Opening up Ruth	Jonathan Prime	978–1–84625–067–5
Opening up Titus	David Campbell	978–1–84625–079–8
Opening up Zephaniah	Michael Bentley	978–1–84625–111–5

About Day One:

Day One's threefold commitment:

- To be faithful to the Bible, God's inerrant, infallible Word;
- To be relevant to our modern generation;
- To be excellent in our publication standards.

I continue to be thankful for the publications of Day One. They are biblical; they have sound theology; and they are relative to the issues at hand. The material is condensed and manageable while, at the same time, being complete—a challenging balance to find. We are happy in our ministry to make use of these excellent publications.

JOHN MACARTHUR, PASTOR-TEACHER, GRACE COMMUNITY CHURCH, CALIFORNIA

It is a great encouragement to see Day One making such excellent progress. Their publications are always biblical, accessible and attractively produced, with no compromise on quality. Long may their progress continue and increase!

JOHN BLANCHARD, AUTHOR, EVANGELIST AND APOLOGIST

Visit our websites for more information and to request a free catalogue of our books.

UK:
www.dayone.co.uk

North America:
www.dayonebookstore.com